Readers' Speak

"An interesting coverage of the HR life cycle for the learning mind in the People Management space. It provides an interesting flavour of the enabling ecosystem and the role a positive culture plays in making people programs succeed in an enterprise. I loved the application-oriented caselets at the end of each theme, which make the book not only interesting for the practitioners but also enchanting for the students of the subject."
—Dr. Adil Malia, Group President - HR, Essar Services India Ltd.

"Reality Bytes – a true ready reckoner by Aparna Sharma succeeds in being a one-stop Human Resources quick-read for students and professionals. She has broken down every concept into crisp modules enriched with caselets that provide practical elements for better understanding. Existing HR professionals can use it in their daily lives to bridge the gap between theory and live aspects of implementation in the workplace. In addition, the questions at the end of every chapter coax the reader to reflect on the strategic role of HR in meeting the business objectives of the organization."
—Rajeev Dubey, President (Group HR, Corporate Services & After-Market) & Member - Group Executive Board, Mahindra & Mahindra Ltd.; National President - NHRDN

"The book 'Reality Bytes' by Aparna brings out the essence of the HR management domain. It covers themes such as Compensation, HR Analytics and Employer & Employee Value Propositions in a succinct manner; topics which hitherto have not been covered well anywhere. This book will serve as an apt initiation book to young managers and aspiring HR professionals. Good work, Aparna!"
—K. Ramkumar, Executive Director, ICICI Bank

"HR professionals are at times accused of using excessive jargon and mumbo jumbo. 'Reality Bytes – The Role of HR in Today's World' is a book that stands out for communicating concepts in a simple and easy to understand manner. The content is simple, not simplistic. This is a book to reach out to, for all professionals who wish to quickly access 101 introductory information on HR. The book packs in a lot of condensed information on various facets of HR, normally not available in one place. The content is contemporary with material on subjects such as HR Analytics, and the caselets make the paperback eminently readable. I am sure that the book is the beginning of the journey of a budding scribe with many more writings on HR."
–Yogi Sriram, SVP (Corporate Human Resources), Larsen & Toubro Limited

"Aparna Sharma's book deals with some very basic issues in HR in a very simple and practical way. This book is a must-read not only for HR professionals but also for students of HR and all the people managers irrespective of their functional areas. It will help HR professionals to see the business side and the business leaders to understand the underlying principles to deal with practical people issues at work. The caselets in the book help the reader to understand live issues and stimulate thinking. The author's wide experience makes these caselets very authentic."
–Satish Kulkarni, CEO & Managing Director - Lhoist India Pvt. Ltd.

"Aparna Sharma's maiden book 'Reality Bytes - The Role of HR in Today's World' encompasses the entire gamut of Employee Life Cycle Management and exhibits profound understanding of the subject. While we know that she is a trained and qualified HR professional, she has displayed her strengths at two distinctly unrelated skills – writing a book in English and Human Resources – with consummate ease, with this book. The range of subject coverage is so wide and comprehensive that any HR professional can happily utilize its learnings as a professional knowledge standard for others to emulate.
I must confess that it is a must-read for all those managing Human Capital and that includes budding HR professionals and those HR students seeking reference books on the subject. The simplicity

and flawless manner in which every aspect of the subject is dealt and also the caselets make the book truly unique.
Wishing Aparna good luck always for the future, and may she pen down many more."
–Anant Rajadnye, General Manager - HR, Masina Hospital TISS - 1972-1974

"Reality Bytes is more than just a good read. The book's universal perspective and strategic approach can guide aspiring managers in their own quest for success. It offers an imaginative and insightful look at what it takes to rise to the top as an HR professional. The book offers abundant tips for all HR leaders looking to transform their organizations. A must-read indeed!"
–Dr. Deepak Deshpande, SVP & Head, HR, Netmagic Solutions

"Your book 'Reality Bytes' is taking me more and more close to the challenging yet interesting subject of HR Management. The concepts like EVP are so well simplified and explained stepwise with caselets and examples which give flawless understanding to the reader about the topic. The book is not only a bible for HR professionals, but also very helpful for Corporate Trainers like me because it perfectly brings me face to face with the scope of soft skills in the HR industry, like the need of training for 'Change Management'. I'm sure this book is going to get included in the list of reference books for Management students very soon. Wishing you good luck and a bright future for penning down many more!!"
–Vrushali Kaul, Corporate Trainer

"It is a pleasure to read 'Reality Bytes', a book on HR Management for practitioners and students alike. It is simple in presentation and content. A good handbook for quick understanding of HR Management at the work place."
–Dr. PLN Raju, Dy. Director (Organizational Effectiveness), The Leprosy Mission Trust India

"'Reality Bytes' is a simple and very effective guide book that every early career HR professional and also managers/professionals who aspire to work with people should have as their ready reckoner. It has been written in a very lucid and engaging language which makes the reading and use of the book much more exciting and a pleasurable experience. The insightful caselets at the end of each of the chapters, provoke deeper thought and help create conceptual clarity - these are certainly the highlights of this great book. The author has very deftly blended theory and practice into a nice work of art which appeals to the heart and mind of every reader."

–Arun S. Kaimal - M.A. in PM & IR, TISS 2007; HR Manager at a Leading Fortune 500 MNC operating in India

"The book 'Reality Bytes' by Aparna has inspired me with a number of great ideas, working in a highly complex and dynamic environment, aiming for sustainability. The learnings from this book are multifold and will help the HR fraternity to manifest all the HR experience with winning ideas for the organization. The comprehensive yet small book outlines the deepest insights into all relevant facets of HR to add value to business in today's highly competitive environment.

The saying of Saint Kabir, 'Gagar Mein Sagar Bharana' (to express a whole lot in very few words) truly befits 'Reality Bytes - The Role of HR in Today's World'. Now it depends on the reader how much water (knowledge) he/she can take to continue as a true partner of business strategy.

Commendable effort, highly recommended!!"

–Umesh Tripathi, Sr. Mgr - HR, UCB India Pvt. Ltd.

"Parachutes and minds work well when they are open. 'Reality Bytes' is a great culmination of knowledge, skill and attitude and it makes people more pragmatic and knowledgeable to understand the dynamics of Human Resources. The caselets provided at the end of every chapter weave practical and theoretical learning. Concepts explained in a simplified manner make this a **must-read** book for all management students, teachers and Human Resource practitioners.

–Dr. Ankush Sharma, COO & Head Management Studies, Vidyalankar Educational Campus

"Life and learning become easier when they are simplified. 'Reality Bytes' is a book which explains HR processes in the most simplified way. The book has covered all aspects of various HR processes in lucid language which helps readers understand it completely. Caselets provided at the end of each chapter are thought-provoking.

This book is a real ready reckoner, not only for HR practitioners but also for entrepreneurs who would like to harness human potential in the right manner.

I wish you the best for future publications!"

–Shridhar Ayyar, AVP - HR, Lafarge India Pvt. Ltd.

"I completed my MBA in Human Resource Management back in 2012. It has been nearly three years, working as an HR professional in a large-scale IT services firm. MBA taught me a lot of HR related concepts but when I actually started working as a HR professional, I realized that theory and reality are very different. There is definitely a gap which I am experiencing.

Having read, 'Reality Bytes - The Role of HR in Today's World', I can confidently say that this book is a wonderful ready reckoner for HR students and young HR professionals like me. The caselets in the book are very interesting and I could relate to them very easily. The book is simple yet highly effective, covering the entire journey of an employee. It reinforces the multiple concepts of HR in a practical manner. Kudos to Aparna for penning down this book and enabling students, young HR professionals and managers to deal with the 'Human' aspects in any organization more effectively."

–Harshit Upadhyay, HR Manager, Large IT Services Company

Reviews & Clippings

Basically, this highly insightful book is about the Management of Human Resources and a good guide for enhancing effective talent management. Sharma has done a great job of writing this book, without jargon to help the newcomers in the field of HR to understand the nuances in HR and its components very easily. Every chapter is written in simple language with illustrations and caselets. The case studies are short and powerful. The presentation of the text and various messages are appealing to any new reader and learner. With this simple book, HR professionals will do their job more systematically than before.
–Afternoon Despatch & Courier

'Reality Bytes - The Role of HR in Today's World' focuses on the management of human resources and how HR contributes to effective talent management. The book, published by Vishwakarma Publications, was launched by Prasad Menon, Chairman, Tata-SIA Airlines, Adil Malia, Group President, HR, Essar Services India Ltd., and Prabir Jha, President and Group CHRO, RIL.
–Mumbai Mirror

Aparna Sharma in Business India
"The single-most competitive edge for any organisation is its people. I have a deep conviction that this is true today and will be in future too. I have covered the entire life-cycle of an employee in any organisation. From recruitment to retention, competency mapping to rewards and, finally, best policies for succession and exit – everything is presented in this book for a student or

manager, employee or employer, to get maximum value and insight into their roles."

Excerpt from Aparna Sharma's interview in Business Manager (businessmanager.in)
BM: What motivated you to write this book when there are crowd of books on HR and people are losing the habit of reading?

Vishwakarma Publications of Pune persuaded me to write a simple, handy book and this request ignited my desire to reach out and help Gen Y, especially the student community who are confused, not sure what HR is, since there are so many preconceived notions.

Formal education in HR does not prepare the young, would-be HR manager or even a line manager who needs to be an HR manager in his/her own right to manage people, to face and deal with the Reality at the Workplace. This book has been written to achieve this very purpose.

This book has something for everyone - whether an HR student, a budding early career HR manager, a line manager, or even a teacher or an entrepreneur trying to understand what HR is all about.

Reality Bytes - The Role of HR in Today's World

A Contemporary Ready Reckoner

Aparna Sharma

VISHWAKARMA
PUBLICATIONS

VP

Reality Bytes - The Role of HR in Today's World

A Contemporary Ready Reckoner

First Edition: March, 2015
Reprint: April, 2015
© Aparna Sharma
For feedback or comments
Email: aparna@aparnasharma.in
www.aparnasharma.in

ISBN No.: 978-93-83572-57-1

Published by:
Vishwakarma Publications
283, Budhwar Peth, Near City Post,
Pune – 411002.
Tel: 020-20261157
Email: info@vpindia.co.in
Website: www.vpindia.co.in

Covers and Designing:
PRAGA Design Studio

Review and Caselets:
Dr. Rajasshrie Pillai

Printed At: Repro India Limited, Mumbai

To GOD, beloved Aai, my family, teachers,
mentors and all those who have
helped me in my professional journey
and quest for learning so far…

Acknowledgements

M y sincere thanks to the many professionals and well-wishers who saw me through this book; all those who provided unconditional support, brainstormed, wrote, helped me with online models and assisted in editing and design.

My humble gratitude to my respected parents, sister, husband and my nephews, Rohit and Ravi Shekhar for their constant encouragement and faith in me.

I would like to thank Mr. Vishal Soni of Vishwakarma Publications, Pune for approaching me with the thought and seeing it to fruition. I appreciate Dr. Rajasshrie Pillai's support with the caselets.

A special mention to my Teachers, Mentors, Senior HR colleagues and all in the HR fraternity who have contributed to my repertoire of experiences in practical and real life learning.

Above all, I would like to thank in advance all my fellow professionals – Aspiring (Management students), Early Career professionals and newly appointed Line Managers for choosing to learn from this ready reckoner.

About the Author

elicitated with the 'HR Super Achiever Award' by Star News at the 20th World HRD Congress 2012, Aparna is a passionate learner in her journey of over 18 years of intense and expansive HR work. In her diverse roles, Aparna has successfully been a learning partner, mentor and coach to leaders, leadership teams and organizations to build competencies, learning abilities and nimbleness for achieving purposeful performance.

After completing her post graduation in Personnel Management & Industrial Relations (PM & IR) from Tata Institute of Social Sciences (TISS), Mumbai, Aparna made her foray into the corporate world through Nocil and moved into different roles in the HR function in organizations like Monsanto, Novartis, UCB, Deutsche Bank and Lafarge. Over the years, Aparna has learnt to persistently and passionately value freedom, authentic relationships and realization of potential of people.

Winner of many accolades like 'Women Leadership Award' for BFSI (Banking, Financial Services & Insurance) Awards by Institute of Public Enterprise (IPE), Hyderabad, 'Achiever of Excellence Award' by Indian Society for Training &

Development (ISTD, Mumbai), '30 Women Achievers Award' by HRD Congress 2013, she has also featured as one of the top women HR Leaders in the country in the anniversary issue of Business Manager, July 2012 and quoted as a Thought Leader in HR. Under her leadership at Lafarge, many in-company Global Awards such as 'Digilearn Championship Trophy' and 'WAVE' (Women Adding Value & Excellence) have been received besides external recognitions like CLO (Chief Learning Officer's) Award consecutively for 3 years.

Beyond her corporate role as an HR Leader, Aparna also dons the hat of HR contributor through her associations with Indian Society of Training & Development (ISTD), All India Management Association (AIMA), National Institute of Personnel Management (NIPM), National HRD Network, and Sumedhas, where she actively participates in disseminating her acquired knowledge and building the HR fraternity by creating future leaders. Currently, she is the Honorary Treasurer of National HRD Network, Mumbai Chapter (2012-2015) and is a member of the Executive Committee. She has also been elected as member of the National Executive Board of NHRDN for the period 2013-2015.

A wildlife enthusiast and an amateur photographer, Aparna spends most of her leisure time close to nature. She also loves travelling as it gives her an opportunity to meet new people. Books are Aparna's favourite friends and she dedicates some time everyday to reading something new. An avid reader, she has a collection of some of the best books of the century.

To know more about Aparna, visit: - www.aparnasharma.in

Foreword

People make things happen and to make things happen they use their talent. People are born talented. People are employed for their talent. Organizations sometimes get so caught up in their systems and processes, targets and results that they end up utilising less and less of the talent of the people they have. Talent or Human Resources have unlimited capacity to expand. It is this talent that leads to building of what is known as intellectual capital of a corporation. As Bill Gates pointed out once, more than 90% of the market capital of many new economy industries particularly in IT and Financial sectors consist of Intellectual Capital, a major component of which is Human Capital. There is no easy way of isolating and measuring it - as it is behind all capital, tangible and intangible.

From the conceptualization of Johari Window, one may say that that there are four parts of our talent:
(i)   Open and public (talent known to self and others);
(ii)   Private or personal (talent known to self only
        and not yet known to others);
(iii)   Blind part (talent noticed by others but not
        known to self); and
(iv)   Dark or unexplored arena (talent that is yet to
        be discovered by self or others and neither known
        to self nor to others).

In our lifetime, we may have discovered only a small part of our talent. In fact, we don't discover most of our talent. By mere logic and reasoning, it appears that with every choice we make, we create a platform for discovering our talent and at the same time close the doors for discovering most of the other talent. For example, the day we chose Science stream we opened the doors to discover our talent in Science but closed the doors for discovering talent in many other fields; Commerce, Economics, Fine Arts, Music etc. Even if we spend our lifetime discovering only our talent we still have left a lot undiscovered as one life is not enough to discover our talent in all fields. When we take up one role, we open a platform to discover our talent in that role but close the doors for talent in other functions.

For the welfare of the human society, we need people who can constantly discover large parts of employee talent and also utilize the same. Organizations are platforms for utilizing existing talent and discovering, nurturing and developing new talent its employees have. The primary purpose of Human Resource Departments is to facilitate talent spotting, development and utilization so that more and more organizational capital is formed. HR managers are therefore Human Capital managers meant to constantly spot, nurture, develop, multiply and utilize talent.

HR Managers are supposed to create the platform and enable processes that make employees discover and utilize their talent. HR people play a very crucial role in making people useful to each other by bringing out the best talent in them and making it available for serving the organization and the society. In recent times, HR has come to centre stage. Many organizations have graduated from the idea of HR as a business partner and strategic partner to HR as the core of the business as intellectual capital builder and HR as an organizational transformer and change manager.

Since humans are the most complex beings, HR managers or those who facilitate talent management need to be highly talented themselves and understand the dynamics of talent management in human resources.

This book is about the Management of Human Resources and a good guide for HR people to do their job well and contribute to effective talent management. Aparna Sharma has done a great job of writing this book without jargon to help the new comers into the field of HR to understand the nuances in HR and its components very easily. Every chapter is written in simple language with illustrations and caselets. The caselets are short and powerful. The presentation of the text and various messages are appealing to any new reader and learner. Using this simple book, we hope HR professionals will do their job more systematically than before.

The book begins with Employer and Employee Value Proposition and covers areas like Talent Acquisition, Development and Management. The book also deals with areas like Competencies, Compensation & Benefits, Organizational Development, Change Management, HR Analytics, Managing Employee Exit and Separation, and Strategic HR. In the last chapter, the author has highlighted Challenges in Today's Human Resource Management. Aparna has done a splendid job of bringing out this book for the new generation HR students, young HR Managers, Line Managers, HR teachers and all those who believe in nurturing human potential and putting the talent of people to use.

I congratulate Aparna for her contribution to the HR profession.

Dr. T. V. Rao
Chairman, TVRLS; and Former Professor, IIMA
Founder President NHRDN
January 21, 2015

Preface

Watching 'Taare Zameen Par' is always a very touching experience for me. This time observing Aamir Khan drive home the point that 'Every Child is Special', I paused to reflect on how very similar this was to my own profession.
'Every individual is special.'

'PEOPLE' are the core of any business. Their talents, skills, ideas and perceptions is what shapes the destiny of organizations. I have been blessed to be part of organizations where this philosophy was not just preached but also practiced. It is what has shaped my career and made me a thorough professional.

Organizations may have the best processes, but it is people who ensure that these processes translate into best practices for overall effectiveness. Otherwise, the best processes remain flowcharts on paper. Although this is not something we are unaware of, this is the most opportune time to recognize that no organization has ever achieved the heights of success without having the right human resources.

The 'Power of Ideas' drives today's world, and ideas are still very individual driven. A team of people with strong ideas needs other members who have the ability to develop those ideas into acceptable concepts and translate them into a successful business road map.

Thus, 'PEOPLE' matter at every stage and level. Successful Human Resource Management is the key factor for businesses and organizations who seek to retain their competitive edge.

As an HR practitioner, as I look back I realize that though people are acknowledged as the most important resource on paper, it is often a challenge for HR managers and organizational policy makers to translate this into *reality*. The reason for this is probably that in spite of a post-graduation in HR, students and would-be managers fall short in understanding or grasping the *reality* that they will face tomorrow. There is often a gap between theory and actual practice. Hence, this book.

Who is this book for?

If you aspire to make your career in HR and want to learn the tricks of the trade even before you start; if you are a foundation student (BBA) studying an introductory module in HRM or a postgraduate management student specializing in HRM; a promising manager or even a management educator, this book offering a practical approach to HR is for YOU.

It follows the logical sequence of an employee's life cycle in any organization. I have attempted to retain a strong practical focus throughout the book, balanced with the right amount of theory for an introductory level. The book covers the various roles that an HR professional plays in today's dynamic world.

This book contains incisive insights and an in-depth analysis of HRM in its many splendid aspects. It is comprehensive and wide-ranging, examining all major aspects of Human Resource Management in a down-to-earth and practical way whilst providing the necessary theoretical underpinning.

I have made a conscious effort to explain the various aspects of Human Resources crisply, with a combination of caselets and examples raising awareness of key issues and challenges involved in HR today.

Throughout, the book lays emphasis on how 'people' are at the centre of an organization and managing people is a vital function, thus highlighting the strategic role that HR plays in attaining the business goals of the organization. The inclusion of simple caselets after each chapter add value for the reader.

I am confident that you will enjoy Reality Bytes and find it useful!

Aparna Sharma
Mumbai, 2015

Contents

1

The Twins

Employer Value Proposition (EVP)
Employee Value Proposition (EVP again)

If you thought a company's customers are only outside it, think again! The company's first customer is its "EMPLOYEE".

Who is an EMPLOYEE?

Putting aside the definition found in dictionaries, an Employee is the most dynamic, the most valuable and the most skilled resource among all the resources of a business. The more dynamic, valuable and skilled a resource, the greater the attention and care it requires to function at its best.

For a HR manager, it is crucial to understand the professional life cycle of an employee. For an organization, not only is it important to attract the right talent, it is also equally important to make sure they are satisfied and remain committed to contributing their best for its business.
But how would the right talent be attracted to your company? Why would they prefer your company over your competition? What would make them stick to your company in spite of lucrative offers elsewhere?

Go down memory lane and you may recollect that even before finishing your graduation, you aspired to be a part of one of the most well-known and respected companies. For some of you, it might have been wanting to work with the Indian multinationals, while others may have wanted to join any of the private sector banking, insurance or telecom companies.

Do you ever wonder what made you aspire to be a part of those companies even before you actually got to know them? What was it about those companies that attracted you to them? What is it that not just draws people to certain organizations but also keeps them committed once they work there?...

What do employees want from an organization?

In my experience the answer to this question is no longer just 'money'. I have found a few other factors that employees hold dear:

1. Satisfaction – Most people would be okay with a pay cut if it means working at something that gives them satisfaction and adds value to their career.

2. Feedback – (Acknowledgement, Appreciation, Reward) – Regular feedback is important to employees; even negative feedback which helps in their development-both personal and professional! An organization must acknowledge the efforts put in by them. In case of good performance, it must ensure that employees are appreciated and rewarded.

3. Growth and Learning – The opportunity to continuously learn something new is high on an employee's priority list.

Once you understand what drives employees, you as an HR manager have ample scope to manage this talent by helping to boost their careers. If you thought a company's customers are only outside it, think again! The company's first customer is its "EMPLOYEE".

There are also some absolute no-no's which makes employees unhappy and dissatisfied. They might even cause you to lose a good employee.

1. No amount of money can keep your employee motivated if he/she feels stuck in a meaningless job.

2. Lack of recognition is another no-no.

3. Probably nothing is as dangerous as the lack of growth and development opportunities.

4. Lack of passion and zest in their leaders – A leader who lacks zest and passion for his/her work makes even the most

performance-oriented employees unhappy.

An organization attracts talent by the way it is perceived by potential employees. In order to attract aspiring employees and retain existing ones, it needs to offer unique benefits that translate into reasons for employees to work for it and give it a competitive advantage. The way a company is perceived by prospective employees can be consciously defined and designed by a company's strategies and policies. This perception is called **Employer Value Proposition (EVP)**, the first TWIN.

An EVP is a unique set of offerings and values that an organization represents for target candidates. It is a long-term strategy that establishes an organization's identity as an employer and differentiates it from its competitors in the employment market.

By analyzing the factors that influence the employer brand, a company can work to define and communicate the EVP. A well-defined EVP, and one which has been communicated with clarity to all stakeholders goes a long way towards creating a strong employer brand. Thus, not only does EVP help to build the long-term foundation of the brand, it also helps to communicate consistent, true, unique and relevant information as well as its values to important target groups. Having a well-defined EVP helps an employer in not having to pay a premium to attract fresh talent. It also means the availability of a larger talent pool for the company and greater employee engagement and satisfaction finally leading to business success.

In my career, I have been blessed to have been part of

organizations where EVP was well-defined, others where we developed it, and still others where we refined the EVP of the organization according to its stakeholders. Such stakeholders are internal employees, ex-employees, recruitment consultants (who help in procuring fresh talent), and communities and organizations the company associates with. All of these are brand ambassadors for the organization.

As an HR professional, there are some questions you need to ask yourself before designing an EVP.

Points to Ponder

1. Where does my company stand as an employer?
2. What is its positioning/image?
3. Can I give a guarantee about my company's value systems and work culture?
4. How do prospective employees look at my company - as a good paymaster, a company with a good work culture, a place with growth opportunities?
5. Are our existing employees happy with the organization? Does it stand up to the perceptions they had before joining us?

Today, an employee has enormous choice (just as your customers do) and what's more, your employee knows it! Just as your customer is informed, so is your prospective employee. He/she is just a click away from information about the organization even before you meet. It is this information and the public perception of your company which decides if this talent will even apply for the position you are so urgently seeking to fill.

Thus, it is very important to have a well-defined, structured **Employer Value Proposition**. But the obvious question is, how does one go about developing it?

> If a company has a properly defined and structured EVP, then it knows exactly what it wants people to feel about it as an employer.

How does an organization develop its EVP statement?

You may have studied the theory of defining an EVP. Now let's look at the approach one should have while developing one.

What do you do when you want to design a new concept? You look for answers to questions like 'What' and 'How'.

Let's take the first question – 'What'. An EVP is basically what people think about your company. It is important to analyze what people say about your organization because the action you take will depend on it. How would you know what is the image of your organization in the minds of people? What do they feel and say about you? If you think finding this is a daunting task, think twice - it's actually not.

Step 1- Start with examining the data/facts you already have. This data is already available in the organization in the form of various sources like exit interviews, employee engagement surveys, on-boarding surveys, recruitment metrics as well as attrition data.

This data needs to be analyzed to change it into meaningful information. Look for patterns, trends, inclinations and movements which show what people feel and think about your organization.

But doing this is just the beginning.

The Twins

Step 2 - For me, God is in the details. When pearl divers look for oysters, they dive in really deep. Even spirituality teaches one to look within, in search of oneself. Of course, while doing so one may encounter some not-so-good facts about oneself. The same may happen with the organization. When this happens, the approach of the senior-most people – the strategy makers in the organization is very important because they will define the strategy and thereby the decisions to be taken.

Here, the stakeholders must choose whether this is going to be an eyewash exercise or give you the true picture of how things are in the company. The DeepDive™ [1] process can include focused group discussions (FGD) which can be clubbed randomly or connected to interviews with key stakeholders.

The purpose of diving deeper is to gain more insight into themes that have been identified through the processes of dissecting data in Step 1.

However, if you wish to have an external face to the EVP, you could use a 'Tell' approach, where the organization tells or specifies what it stands for. So the EVP will be defined as an answer to the question, 'How does this organization deliver the brand promise through its products and services?'

However, an employee-centric approach is the best in defining EVP because not only is it aligned to existing HR strategies, which are in turn aligned to the business strategies of the company, but it also includes the voice of the employees.

Step 3 - Now that you have reached a stage where you have

Source: (1) (http://www2.deloitte.com/us/en/pages/operations/solutions/deepdive-team-toolkit.html)
The DeepDive process is a trademark owned by Deloitte.

a clear understanding of the EVP, you can go on to actually developing the EVP in tandem with the HR strategy of the company. Make sure it focuses on important areas like Employee Engagement, growth, career development, work-life balance etc.

It must be a simple and comprehensive statement encompassing the essence of the employee experience and the employer brand commitment. Thus, though EVP needs to be experiential, it also needs to be a concrete statement similar to the Vision and Mission statements of a company.

Step 4 - With the communication of the EVP, the process of defining the EVP gets completed. This communication has to be across all employee experiences beginning from the recruitment process, on-boarding, career development, right up to the exit stage. Thus, communicating the EVP covers the entire employee life cycle.

While communicating the EVP, you need to ensure that the EVP message and intent is delivered through all mediums like recruitment advertisements, updates on the company intranet, other internal communication, company posters, danglers, company videos etc.

Step 5- Finally, the last step of communicating the EVP is developing systems to measure EVP by integrating it into employee surveys and people metrics. Doing so, will help to demonstrate the value of the EVP, calculate return on investment and the financial benefit to the organization. [2]

Business Strategy, HR Strategy and EVP –
Let us understand that the HR strategy of any organization is based on its business strategy. Do you recollect Adam

Smith's statement on 'Invisible hands' where he propagates the theory that market forces of demand and supply are invisible?

Business is driven and sustained by the demand for its products and services by customers. Naturally, an organization would design its business strategy accordingly. Its HR strategy and in turn its EVP would be defined accordingly.

So EVP is linked to the HR strategy, which is in turn linked to the organization's Business Strategy.

EVP will differ as per the industry, the product and the market segment that a company wishes to target. However, there are still some universal qualities which a good EVP must have. Though you may have read about them, let's revise how a good EVP should be.

What makes a Good EVP?
1. As we saw, an organization's HR strategy goes hand-in-hand with its business strategy. The EVP goes hand-in -hand with the HR strategy. Therefore, a good EVP must reflect how strong and impactful your HR strategy is.
2. A good EVP is the reason people are going to be attracted to your organization. Therefore, it needs to be unique.
3. To give the organization optimum returns, it should be defined around the right characteristics. It should also specify growth and development opportunities for employees.
4. Completely aligned to the organization's business strategy, your EVP should be clear enough to attract and retain the talent required.
5. A large part of your EVP must be true in the 'here and now'. It should be frank about what your organization can

offer to employees as of now.

6. At the same time, your EVP should also have elements that aren't true yet, but are a part of the organization's aspirations. It should also   highlight what changes your organization would like to incorporate in itself in the future. Employees prefer an organization which is open to change and is adaptable.

7. Lastly, an EVP should be designed such that it would appeal to your target group.

The features of the EVP must surely reflect in the corporate brand and the employer service brand.

This would answer the question 'How'.

Of equal importance is the next phase, penetration of the EVP or communication of the EVP message across the organization and across all the stages of the Employee Life Cycle. How the message reaches the employees is essential because if the EVP is not communicated effectively, everything is lost.

> In today's world it is a challenge for companies to differentiate their EVP from others. Though some may take advantage of branding to achieve this, if it doesn't reflect reality, it has an adverse effect.

The Twins

EVP is at the heart of the Employee's Corporate Voyage

Legend -

2. Corporate Brand,
3. Organization Strategy,
4. Organization Structure,
5. Employer Brand,
6. HR Strategy,
7. Internal Communication,
8. Recruitment,
9. Employee Engagement.

Impact of the EVP on your organization

A good EVP shows the organization what is important for the people who work or wish to work for it. Your work as a HR manager begins from here – making efforts to ensure that the right talent gets the justice it deserves.

This process helps you to understand your HR priorities and prioritize your HR agenda. Good EVP's take into account all the workforce needs to create a universal brand which is then communicated through the best channel for each segment. Most companies with a good EVP do not have to engage in the war for talent and pay a premium to attract it. Skilled talent is almost always attracted to them.

A good EVP is the driver of employee engagement, recruitment and retention. For business overall, an EVP has a strong positive impact on Return on Investment throughout the Employee Life Cycle.

> To sum it up, Employer Value Proposition is branding the organization to its prospective employees.

Now let's meet the other TWIN:

Employee Value Proposition - (EVP) again
This time round it's about what the company expects of employees in turn for the compensation, benefits, work culture, growth etc. that it provides. It's like the other side of the same coin. It's important to define what you, as an employee can contribute to the employer.

> Employee Value Proposition is what the employee brings to the organization when he/she joins and continues to hone as well as develop as he/she grows in the organization.

While employees are the most important asset of an organization, manpower is also the largest component of a company's expenditure. When companies invest in employees they expect better outcomes/results from them. Placement ads too use terms like 'result-oriented, impactful and responsible' to describe candidates they are looking for.

The Twins

So, what does an organization expect from its employee?

An organization needs people who can align their career goals with its business goals. The very basic expectations of a company from an employee are the basic values of honesty, reliability and responsibility. Further on, the company expects that the candidate will be aligned to its values, culture and support its long-term goals. An employee must utilize his/her skills for the benefit of the organization. He/she should stand out as an example of hard work, dynamism and take on challenges which can help the company grow.

Companies which have a strong EVP
- Can acquire the right talent
- Will have lesser attrition and retention issues with reference to highly skilled employees
- Will report considerably higher financial results than others in their industry
- Will have employees with high levels of engagement

The Connect Between the TWINS -

We have seen the contribution of these twins to the growth of the organization. Like identical twins, there is a strong alignment between Employer Value Proposition and Employee Value Proposition. The proper balance between the two will ensure that the organization attracts and retains the right talent, and ensures their satisfaction, ultimately leading to an increase in the productivity of employees.

Basically, Employer Value Proposition and Employee Value Proposition are two sides of the same coin. While one side pictures the brand's point of view, the other side shows you the employee's point of view. The perfect tuning between the employees' goals and company's goals give sustainable results.

Soulful music resonates only when the instrument is well-tuned. Similarly, only if Employer Value Proposition and Employee Value Proposition are well tuned, can the brand achieve sustainable growth. If the musician is given a well-tuned instrument naturally the audience would expect a superlative performance from him and that's natural.

That's how these twins are and need to be – interdependent, compatible and inseparable! Proper alignment between them ensures attracting and retention of the right talent, and guarantees its satisfaction, ultimately leading to increase in overall employee productivity and increased business performance.

Thus, you have a very important role as an HR manager to achieve this end.

■■■

The Twins

Caselet I

Exclusive Media was a media company well-known for its work in the regional language of the state. Due to its grass root level connections, it had a very good reputation among media professionals in the state. It had about 30 odd people who had all begun their careers with Exclusive and had never worked anywhere else. Though only some of them were graduates, all of them had grown up with the company, were nurtured there, were skilled at their jobs and good at getting things done – a major requirement in a small company.

The promoters decided to expand and take in new people. Candidates who came in for interviews were MBA's, were tech savvy and could speak good English. With a view to expand Exclusive's business, the promoters decided to recruit such candidates.

Accordingly, a team of 10 new people was recruited for Marketing and Sales. However, things went wrong from day one. The new employees who had worked for MNC's earlier found that such systems were non-existent in Exclusive. The older employees preferred to directly speak to the promoters themselves instead of going through their new bosses. All the older employees, though at junior positions knew much more about the business than the new employees at senior positions and they continued to follow their earlier systems.

From the new employees' point of view, they were taken aback by the difference in the company's way of operation and what they were used to. Also, Exclusive was dealing with vendors, associates and customers from remote areas of the state and the well-qualified, English speaking sales people were not even familiar with the regional language.

All-in-all, there was a complete mismatch of the expectations of the company and the expectations of the newcomers. This led to conflicts within teams, (Old Vs. New) such that it adversely affected Exclusive's business.

The promoters finally consult a HR expert – YOU, to find out what went wrong.

What you need to work on:
1. Identify the problem in this caselet.
2. Finding ways to address the problem identified.
3. The 3 measures you would use to address this problem.
4. The advice you would give the company as a HR consultant, so that this problem does not arise in the future.

Caselet II

Shiva was working with KT Pvt. Ltd. for the last ten years. Then the company went through hard times and shut down a few operating units, including Shiva's, for cutting costs. After losing his job, Shiva easily got another job at JW Pvt. Ltd., due to his experience and expertise. After a few weeks of working there, while relaxing on the weekend, he reflected on his tenure at KT Pvt. Ltd.

Shiva had been in love with his earlier job and had been a part of the team from day one. KT Pvt. Ltd. had helped him to achieve his personal goals and met his expectations fully. Shiva had grown in the organization and his work had been appreciated and recognized. He had received four promotions and many monetary rewards. Shiva liked the decentralization of authority and KT had allowed him considerable autonomy and freedom. The culture at KT was employee friendly and communication was open. Everybody in KT was aware of what was going on in the organization.

People at the workplace were very nice. Shiva and other managers went out together to lunches and played cricket every Saturday. Everybody got along well, both personally and professionally and worked as a team always. The bosses too were very supportive and had helped employees as and when needed.

When the KT unit shut down, Shiva was devastated as he was sure nothing could replace KT. After spending few weeks at JW Pvt. Ltd., as Shiva reflected on the comparison between KT and JW, he was disturbed for various reasons.

At JW, the managers did not care who did a good job and who didn't. JW promoted and rewarded employees based on how long they had been with the organization and how well they played the political game.

JW was bureaucratic and authority was centralized. Managers were too busy giving memos and getting signatures from senior management. He found that nobody was ready to mingle personally and professionally with each other.
In consideration of the above, Shiva felt that he had made a mistake by taking up the job at JW.

What you need to work on:
1. What was the Employer Value Proposition at KT Pvt. Ltd. that Shiva had experienced?
2. What are the reasons why Shiva feels he made a mistake by joining JW?
3. What will you do if you are Shiva?

2

The 3 'T's':

- Talent Acquisition
- Talent Development
- Talent Management

't' + 't' = 'T'

In our childhood, we learnt 'T' for table or 'T' for telephone. But in HR, 'T' is for TALENT.

An employee's 'Talent' is the most fundamental need for the organization to achieve its goals. Every employee tries to align his/her talent to better his/her performance and achieve organizational goals, else the organization aligns employees with specific talent to fulfill its needs. It can work both ways. As we saw in the last chapter, Employer Value Proposition and Employee Value Proposition act like compatible twins in HR Management. Talent is the base for both these concepts.

Right Talent Acquisition, Talent Development and Talent Management in its true sense is the most critical expectation and function of HR in today's times. It's also the ultimate challenge for HR today.

Let's first understand what Talent is. As per McKinsey, "Talent is the sum of A person's abilities + His/her intrinsic gifts + Skills, knowledge, experience + Intelligence + Judgement + Attitude + Character + Drive + His/her ability to learn and grow."

TALENT according to me is as follows:
• 'T' stands for TOLERANT. It is important to be tolerant and not say no for any kind of work. There is learning for an employee in every job undertaken.
• 'A' stands for ASPIRE. It is important to have aspirations in life in order to reach the pinnacle of an employee's chosen field.
• 'L' stands for LEARN. Every employee must always be open

to learning in every aspect of life. Life is a teacher and so it is important to have an open mind.

• 'E' stands for EXPERIMENT. An employee should believe in coming out of his/her comfort zone and trying something new in order to achieve success.

• 'N' stands for NOBLE. It is important that an employee is noble in his/her deeds and not self-centered. This way, he/she will not only think of himself/herself but of the organization as a whole.

• 'T' stands for TRUST. An employee should be extremely trustworthy and reliable.

Now you may be wondering what the title of this chapter – 't' + 't' = 'T' means?

An organization's success is heavily dependent on its people. So, it all begins with having the right person for the right job. After the first step of defining Employer and Employee Value Propositions, the next step with regards to talent is Talent Acquisition. Needless to say, Acquisition needs to be followed by Talent Development. If you club both the above mentioned steps, what you get is the whole - Talent Management.

Simplistically put, that's the equation:

't' (Talent Acquisition) + 't' (Talent Development) = 'T' (Talent Management)

Let us look at each 't' and 'T' in greater detail to understand how do they finally add up.

Talent Acquisition (t) –
Getting the right people

Talent Acquisition is a strategic function referring to identifying, assessing and hiring skilled people for organizational needs. Not only does it include talent procurement, but also workforce planning functions such as talent forecasting, assessment and development.

The needs of recruitment - hiring and attracting top talent have led to the development of talent acquisition as a career. A talent acquisition professional needs to be skilled at sourcing, candidate assessment, compliance and hiring standards, employment branding practices as well as corporate hiring initiatives.

Talent Acquisition has now also become closely aligned with Marketing & Public Relations besides Human Resources. Very often you will find that it is the Talent Acquisition professionals who craft the Employer Value Proposition around the company's hiring approach and the ongoing development of employees. The employment brand therefore embraces not only the procurement of human capital, but also the approach to corporate employee development.

This is what the general process of Talent Acquisition looks like:

Recruiting - Sourcing

⬇

Talent Assessment - Screening

⬇

Talent Selection - Hiring

⬇

Pre-boarding

⬇

On boarding

1) Recruiting – Getting the Right People – In order to find the manpower you require, you first need a clear Job Description (JD) which includes - the job title, to whom the job reports, duties and responsibilities, the purpose and scope of the job, expected standards of performance and the working conditions of a job. A Job Description becomes the basis for the Job Specification which is a statement of the qualifications and characteristics an employee must have to perform the tasks required for the job.

The following is the recruitment process that is generally followed:

i) Developing the criteria for selection - The JD will help you ensure that the selection criteria are measurable so that interviews are objective and there is no bias. Check for two sets of criteria – employee based and organization based. Employee based criteria would be skill sets, expertise, experience etc. Organization based criteria would be the person's compatibility with the organizational culture and structure etc., the impact of this person on others in the organization and their attitude, compatibility of the job with the team etc.

ii) Choosing the right recruitment methods - Recruiting for skilled positions is highly competitive giving rise to the need for creativity to attract the right talent. There is a need to think out of the box.

The oldest management guru of India, Chanakya had advised rulers to look for slightly older farmers with fallow fields as their spies! Since their fields were fallow, they weren't very busy and were happy with the compensation. Also, since they were farmers, no one suspected them and they collected a lot of information this way.

The HR manager can choose among various methods of recruitment like Internal Job Postings, Print Ads, Placement Agencies, Walk-ins, Employee Referrals and Career Fairs as per their suitability for their organizations.

Now let's look at some of the newer and popular methods of recruitment.

a. Internal Job Posting (IJP) –
Internal Job Posting (IJP) is a method for Internal Recruitment. Its main objective is to provide an opportunity to the employee to apply for an internal job vacancy based on opportunities created by business conditions and considering the employee's work-related performance and job-related qualifications in accordance with the company policy.

IJP permits the organization to match its continuous needs for competent personnel with the desire of employees to advance and apply the skills and knowledge developed in order to achieve organizational efficiency and effectiveness. It enables cross movements in order to gain diverse work experience. It also provides employees with opportunities for job enrichment and job rotation.

The potential benefits of this approach are that the management already has a good idea of the employee's capabilities. It acts as a reward for the employee's past performance while giving him/her an opportunity for career development. An organization can retain its investment in the employee by using this method. The time and costs of recruitment and orientation are reduced. It also generates a positive morale and retention by signaling the possibility of internal progression.

However, if used in isolation, it provides a limited number of people to select from. Similarly, the diversity within the organization is reduced. A big drawback of this method is that employees applying for the position who are not selected may be disgruntled. Hence, closing the loop with constructive feedback is very important for employees to continue to have faith in the process and system.

b. Online recruiting – This is an older but very popular method of recruitment. Jobsites like Naukri.com, Monster.com, Timesjobs.com etc., are popular for the convenience and ease of use. A recent study shows that 96% of the people looking for jobs use the internet. Here's a checklist for a good response for your job posting.

• Clear Job Title – Be specific. E.g. Mention Manager - Admin. instead of just Manager.
• Use of Key Words – Use words and phrases commonly used to describe the job.
• Precise information for the web - Use highlighting and headings (e.g. About Us, How to Apply etc.)

c. Mobile Recruiting
Mobile recruiting is a dynamic and growing industry with over 19% job seekers using mobile devices to search for jobs. Mobile Recruiting means finding candidates actively and passively by using mobile career pages and internet recruiting strategies through social platforms.

Mobile technology has completely changed the job search and hiring process. Today, candidates apply using mobile apps. Recruiters can also now tap candidates who are passively job searching as they browse their devices throughout the day. Many companies have developed mobile recruitment strategies to adapt to this change in candidate behavior.

d. Networking and Liaison

This involves reaching out to your existing network for recommendations. This could also involve efforts to build or increase your current network to connect with new potential employees.

The advantage is that candidates reached through an existing network may have some prior knowledge of the organization or the sector. When you increase your network, it can have many organizational benefits beyond your current recruitment needs, such as volunteer recruitment, increased awareness and visibility in the community, etc. However, relying solely on this method might decrease the diversity of your organization.

iii) Develop the Job Posting/Advertisement - How the job posting/advertisement is projected to prospective employees is important. Needless to say, basic information like qualifications, job title, work profile, experience required, skills and personal attributes, etc. will no doubt be a part of the advertisement. But besides that, like any other advertisement, this advertisement too has to clearly project the image/profile of your organization and its branding thereby creating a positive perception among the prospective employees. It should give an indirect trust and faith about their career progress.

It should guide employees on how they should go about applying for the job. The format, wording, layout and design of the advert should be consistent with your organization's style and brand and should also have your company logo.

The 3 'T's:

An organization advertising for a technical post found a remarkable way of getting the right candidates interested in their firm. The company designed their ad such that it would increase the curiosity of the candidates, yet filter them based on their skills. For this purpose, they used a QR code. A QR code consists of black modules (square dots) arranged in a square grid on a white background, which can be read by an imaging device (such as a camera). The candidates had to answer a technical question which was placed inside the QR code printed in the ad which the candidates were supposed to scan with their smartphones. Only on answering that question would the candidates be eligible for the further process. Thus, the company ensured that only candidates who had these skills and a techno-savvy mindset would apply.

QR Code

iv) Attracting Candidates - When thinking about features of the job or your organization that will attract candidates, consider points like the work culture, career path, development opportunities, how meaningful the job is etc.

Make sure that the picture you put up about your organization is not only attractive but absolutely true - else, it can lead to problems including candidates not accepting an offer, or worse, leaving after only a few months.

2) Talent Assessment
This is the next step after Recruitment in the process of Talent Acquisition. It refers to analyzing the incoming talent

against a talent profile which has been developed by the company. These assessments may be used for multiple purposes and should be used as a guide in the overall process.

3) Talent Selection

> Ensuring employee delight, safety, tight budgets, running lean etc are among the numerous challenges organizations face. All these goals can only be accomplished with the help of highly skilled employees.

Remember, the final objective is to hire highly skilled talent which fits into your organizational culture.

Science of Selection –

Leading organizations have adopted Selection Science to identify, source, qualify and hire individual employees who can be a good long-term fit. Each company has different methods of selection for various needs. The most common methods are Online test (Technical/Non-technical) followed by Group Discussion and Personal Interviews.

To ensure a higher level of care to employees, organizations should consider implementing the following four best practices of Selection which are:

i. Behavioral-based interviewing – This refers to analyzing an employee's behavioral pattern from the past. Organizations make use of effective questions to explore key job-related behaviour from past employment or even academic situations in case of freshers.

For example, an applicant may be asked to describe the

learnings from his/her previous job. Follow-up questions could include asking exactly what the individual did in this situation, what motivated their actions and what the outcome was.

ii. Stress interviewing - As the name suggests this practice is used by employers to subject candidates to intense pressure to check how they perform. The main purpose is to find out how a candidate handles stress, work overload, how they deal with multiple projects and how good they are at handling workplace conflict.

iii. Create hiring teams - To avoid biased hiring decisions by a single interviewer, a good solution is to create an interviewing team of multiple interviewers. Ideally the team should have 3-5 people (team-mates and supervisors). The advantages of this method are that existing employees feel that their inputs are considered for team development and the new hires are more likely to be supported by their teammates if peers were involved in their selection.

iv. Standardize processes to align the team - To remove bias, another method used is creating standardized hiring processes. It means measuring applicant competencies in the same way each time for every applicant. This requires a standardized process of asking the same questions from interview to interview, using higher-quality questions(such as behavior based), and evaluating the answers in a standard way.

4) Pre-boarding
From the time a new employee accepts your offer to join and his/her first day, there is generally little or no contact between the company and employee. During this period

(Pre-Boarding) he/she is most susceptible to finding a new employer or opportunity. That is why engagement and interaction with him/her is of utmost importance.

Pre-boarding engages the new hire by providing company information, product lines, initial staff orientation, information on benefits and especially networking opportunities with new colleagues. It also delivers training and development to a new hire and laying the groundwork for the first day on the job. It helps to pair the new employee with a buddy to help him/her "learn the ropes".

5) On boarding
In many organizations, this process is owned by the Learning & Development function. Additionally, as the role of Talent Acquisition has become more strategic, many organizations also encompass Workforce Planning in Talent Acquisition. Workforce Planning is treated as a supporting process and its associated measures are not included in the Talent Acquisition process. In practice, every organization is free to organize their HR activities any way they choose.

However, a framework is surely needed to organize the measures.

Once the employee joins, he needs to have a complete orientation to settle and grow into the organization. Employee Orientation is the process of providing new employees with basic background information about the firm. Employee Orientation should be based on the following criteria –
a. The businesses the company is in
b. The basis on which it will compete and
c. The traits and skills that employees need, to achieve the

organization's strategic goals.[1]

Nurturing Diversity in Talent Acquisition- To ensure the selection of diverse talent, HR policies and practices should be reviewed carefully to identify barriers (like discrimination and stereotyping) and opportunities for improvement in the recruitment and selection process. Being an Equal Opportunity Employer is not a fad. Equally important is valuing differences between people and understanding the positive benefits of employing a diverse range of talented people.

A positive approach to diversity allows you to select the best person for the job based on merit alone and free from bias based on age, physical disability, gender, sexual orientation or race that in no way affect the person's ability to do the job. Employers that take this approach are more likely to be seen as a fair, positive and progressive place to work by the diverse society that they are part of.

Every employee is unique. Only if employers take diversity seriously can they recruit, retain and develop the talent needed to improve performance and to sustain.

Talent Development (t)

Once we complete the step of Talent Acquisition, we need to move on to the next step that is developing this talent for the organization.

• **Learning & Development –** It is next on the agenda after Employee Orientation i.e. once the employee settles and starts performing in the organization. In today's jargon, L&D is equivalent to Training. Learning and Development

Source: (1) https://www.centerfortalentreporting.org/talent-acquisition/

(L&D) strategy is an organizational strategy that outlines the capabilities, skills or competencies required by the workforce to ensure that the organization is sustainable and successful and puts in place the means of developing these capabilities to strengthen organizational effectiveness.

The Learning and Development strategy should reflect, reinforce and be aligned to the approach within the broader HRM strategy and also link with other strategies (for example, Reward & Recognition – R&R).

An organization's learning strategy should focus on:
I. Enhancing performance of average performers and
ii. Helping high-performing or high-potential individuals (whose contribution is critical to long-terms business success) to further develop their skills.

4 Steps of Training:
1. Training Needs Identification
2. Training Needs Analysis
3. Training Plan
4. Training Calendar

1. Training Needs Identification (TNI) –

It is a tool utilized to identify the training to be provided to employees to improve their work productivity. To make a difference, it should focus on the needs as opposed to desires of the employees. Training need identification should be based on:-
• Whether it will make a difference to the productivity and the bottom line.
• The training requirements of each employee and what will improve his/her job performance.
• Matching organizational goals and individual aspirations.

The 3 'T's:

Identification of training needs is important for an organization because it has objectives that it wants to achieve for the benefit of all stakeholders such as owners, employees, customers, suppliers, etc. These objectives can be achieved only through harnessing the abilities of its people, releasing potential and maximizing opportunities for development.

Therefore, employees must know what they need to learn in order to achieve organizational goals. To meet aspirations of employees, the organization must provide effective and attractive learning resources and conditions. And it is also important to see that there is a suitable match between achieving organizational goals and providing attractive learning opportunities.

Different Levels for conducting TNI-
Identification of training needs can be done at three levels to ascertain three kinds of needs : [2]
• Organizational Needs - Whether the organization is meeting its current performance standards and objectives, if and when a major new strategy is to be adopted, a new product or service is to be created, while undergoing a large-scale change programs or developing new relationships like new partnerships etc.
• Group Needs - Information about the group performance (a team, a department, function, sub-unit etc.) may identify areas of need - which, again, may be for training or other interventions.
• Individual Needs - This is about finding out to what extent individuals need to learn or be trained so that their current performance comes up to the required level with the help of changes in methods and processes that require new competencies and skills.

Source: (2) http://www.pmiralumni.co.in

It helps to find out whether individuals are comfortable in working across boundaries, with people from different backgrounds and different perspectives. This is especially important since there is so much workforce diversity observed today in organizations that it has become almost impossible to retain workforce, which is not flexible enough to accommodate such changes in their daily work schedule.

2. Training Needs Analysis (TNA)

This analysis should be conducted at all the above three levels to ensure the maximum return from training and skills throughout the organization. It points out the gap between the required level of skill/knowledge and the current level of skill/knowledge and the most appropriate training to bridge this gap. The techniques used would include SWOT (Strengths, Weaknesses, Opportunities and Threats) analysis, one-to-one interviews and SMART (Specific, Measurable, Attainable, Realistic & Time-bound) objectives.

3. Training Plan

The training plan will outline who will deliver the training, and when and where the training will take place. A training plan should be flexible enough to meet all the needs of the organization. It must specify-
• the competencies that employees need to obtain
• the time frame for achieving them
• the training to be undertaken
• the delivery modes to be employed
• responsibility for delivery and/or assessment of each competency.

4. Training Calendar

Training calendars are ideal for training which is regularly required, for example, soft skills like communication, time

The 3 'T's:

management, or refresher training and also training for new recruits.

Benefits of Employee Learning and Development include:
• Employees are better prepared and motivated to help the organization achieve its goals
• Staff are more productive and require less supervision
• A pool of employees are ready to replace others who leave
• Staff are better able to meet the challenges of changes in the organization
• Staff are able to manage/work on new programs
•Organization will be more successful at attracting and retaining employees

Creating a learning environment -
The learning environment provided by an organization is a function of the organizational culture. Organizational culture means the values, attitudes and beliefs reflected in the mission, goals, and practices of the organization.

Here are some ways organizations that value learning provide a supportive learning environment:

1. Recognize that learning is part of everything the organization does - Opportunities to learn happen all the time. Organizational cultures that support learning recognize learning as an ongoing process, not an event.

2. Support the expectation of learning with resources - An organization shows that it values learning by including employee learning and development in the annual budgeting process. Items included in the annual budget reflect the priorities of the organization.

3. Encourage learning at all levels - Opportunities to learn are made available for everyone in the organization from the Board of Directors to the most junior staff.

4. Recognize that mistakes are learning opportunities - One way an organization shows that it values learning, is in its approach to mistakes. Encourage people to learn from mistakes rather than being afraid to admit their mistakes for fear of disciplinary action.

5. Allow for practice of new skills on-the-job - Learning does not end when the activity is over. Opportunities to use the knowledge and skills they have learned on-the-job will ensure that people retain what they have learned.[3]

What is a Career Path?

A career path is the sequence of positions or roles that a person holds over the span of his work life. Career paths may be planned or unplanned and can include a number of positions. They can be upward, lateral, and downward (as defined by pay or status) moves. They can be within a single organization (which is increasingly uncommon) or several organizations; within a single industry or several industries or career fields.

An employee needs to take an honest look at his/her career goals, skills, knowledge, experience, and personal characteristics. He/she should have a plan to obtain what is necessary in each of these areas to carry out his or her career path. Employees must have flexible career plans to understand the skills through which they can achieve their career goals, and to pursue career development opportunities within the organization to make their dreams a reality.

Career Path and Employee Retention

In a recent survey released by the Society for Human Resource Management (SHRM) and CareerJournal.com,

Source: (3) http://hrcouncil.ca/hr-toolkit/learning-ready.cfm

employees cite three main reasons for their exit - over 50% specify better compensation and benefits, 35% specify problems in their current career path, and 32% need new challenges.

Today's job market is becoming an increasingly competitive environment. If you want your employees to be in for the long haul, they must believe that their organization supports and values their career goals.

Career Development Planning is critical for Employee Retention!

Almost all organizations know that they cannot depend only on attractive perks and compensation to attract talent and retain employees. Smart employees are more likely to be influenced by a clear growth plan or a career path. A proper career path shows employees that you are investing in them and value their development. This helps to nurture a better relation between the employees and the company. These employees will be the best brand ambassadors for the organization.

There are three types of Career Paths:

1. Vertical Career Path – With the importance that promotions and titles (vertical movement) carry in the business world, no doubt your employees will be motivated to earn promotions and move up in title and responsibilities including higher compensation.

2. Horizontal Career Path - Horizontal movement occurs across different departments or department locations within a company, usually at the same level with comparable responsibilities. For example, a transfer to a different region, or from marketing to sales.

3. Lateral Career Path - A lateral career path is a job change with different responsibilities, while the job title remains the same. The level of responsibility is similar in the new position. Moving laterally offers benefits like new skills, new experiences and business knowledge, and interaction with new people.

Leadership Development

Every position needs an able successor. Successors are not born, they are developed. Developing the next generation of leaders is a key task. The organization needs to identify high performers and design plans for them to ensure their development.

I recommend creating in-house leadership development programs that single out so-called high-potential employees and put them through multi-year programs, including mentorships, management classes, stretch assignments and coaching. The goal is to elevate candidates above a single function and give them a broader vision of the company.

Following are the commonly deployed ways to develop leaders:
1. Rotate people through different jobs
2. Challenge them with unfamiliar jobs
3. Ensure frequent feedback and coaching for them
4. Send them for International programs

Career Interviews

A career interview is a dedicated meeting between an employee and the HR Manager. The meeting's objective is to align organizational and individual needs and capabilities in developing talents. It is not just talking about job moves.

The 3 'T's:

The career interview's goal is to:
- review current and earlier activities and professional skills of the employee
- understand the individual's strengths and areas that need improvement
- identify directions of professional development for the individual
- examine possibilities for an individual development plan, taking into account the individual's preferences and the prospects that the company can offer
- confirm engagement levels and incorporate feedback along with support required on development needs in the talent management strategy

Talent Management (T)

Remember, we derived the equation : 't'+"t'= 'T'
This 'T' stands for Talent Management.

Talent Management is an on-going end to end process of planning, recruiting, developing, managing, compensating and retaining talented employees throughout the Employee Life Cycle in the organization. Employees are not just selected for the right jobs but are also nurtured through training, and continuously monitored and coached for performance. It presents one of the most challenging tasks as part of the HR strategy.

You must have understood by now that 'Talent' is an ornament that the organization adorns itself with. Needless to say, it must be treated that way.

Clear EVP - Recruiting right people for right jobs - Talent Acquisition

Clear Business Goal – Training, Career Path - Talent Development

Organizational Strategy - Employee retention plan - Talent Management

Talent Management is an organization's pledge to recruit, develop and retain talented employees. All the processes and systems related to recruiting, developing and retaining a superior workforce would come under the scope of Talent Management.

Talent Management is a business strategy and must be fully integrated within all of the employee related processes of the organization. Talent Management is the job of every member of the organization, not just managers who have staff (talent) reporting to them. An effective strategy for Talent Management is to share information about talented employees and their potential career paths across the organization enabling various departments to identify available talent when opportunities arise.

Assessment of Talent Potential

Talent Management would first aim at assessing which employees are talented and can be developed and retained by the organization to achieve its business goals. An important step here is that of Potential Assessment. Here is a commonly used and extremely effective tool to assess talent in organizations, also referred to as "The Nine Box" Model.

The 3 'T's'

9 Box Performance-Potential Matrix

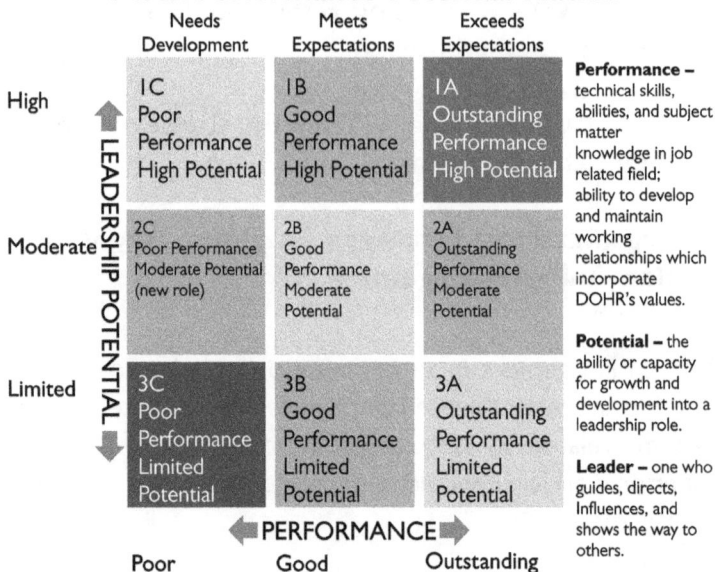

	Needs Development	Meets Expectations	Exceeds Expectations
High	1C Poor Performance High Potential	1B Good Performance High Potential	1A Outstanding Performance High Potential
Moderate	2C Poor Performance Moderate Potential (new role)	2B Good Performance Moderate Potential	2A Outstanding Performance Moderate Potential
Limited	3C Poor Performance Limited Potential	3B Good Performance Limited Potential	3A Outstanding Performance Limited Potential

LEADERSHIP POTENTIAL

◄ PERFORMANCE ►

| Poor | Good | Outstanding |

Performance – technical skills, abilities, and subject matter knowledge in job related field; ability to develop and maintain working relationships which incorporate DOHR's values.

Potential – the ability or capacity for growth and development into a leadership role.

Leader – one who guides, directs, Influences, and shows the way to others.

D✹HR

It is widely used in Succession Planning and Development. It assesses individuals on two dimensions – their 'past' performance and their 'future' potential.

The X axis (horizontal line) assesses leadership performance while the Y axis (vertical line) assesses leadership potential. A combination of X and Y axis makes up the box within the grid that the leader is placed. This matrix helps demarcate employees into 1A - High Performance/High Potential, 3C - Low Performance/Low Potential, etc.[4]

The focus of Talent Management should be on nurturing High-Potential Talent.

High-Potential Talent – They are the talent pool of future

Source: (4) http://www.greatleadershipbydan.com/2012/01/performance-and-potential-matrix-9-box.html

organizational leaders. They have the ability, commitment and motivation to rise and be successful in more senior positions in the organization and aim to have a fast track career. They usually grow fast and achieve success at a young age.

Succession Planning

Let's try to answer some questions:
• How can a company develop and nurture its human capital?
• How can you be sure of having qualified people take over important positions when the existing managers and key people retire or move on?
• How can you plan for the future of the company without this assurance?

The answer to these questions is Succession Planning. Succession Planning is a continuous process where an organization ensures that employees are recruited and developed to fill each key role within the company. While organizations go through the cycles of expansion, increase in volumes, providing opportunities for career growth, creation of new jobs - employee promotions, transfers, organizational restructuring and losing people to competition – effective and proactive succession planning ensures that there is never a dearth of talented employees to take up necessary roles that come up.

Through the Succession Planning Process, superior employees are recruited, their knowledge skills and abilities are developed and they are prepared for more challenging roles. One may think that Succession Planning is only for large conglomerates or family-owned businesses but ideally, it should be part of every company's Strategic Plan.

The 3 'T's:

In the earlier step, we have assessed the high-potential employees we require for our Succession Plan. Now, they need to be developed and groomed. This can be undertaken through well-known practices such as:
a) Lateral Moves,
b) Special Project Assignments,
c) Team Leadership roles, and both
d) Internal and external training and development opportunities.

Do's for Effective Succession Planning in your organization

1. Identify the organization's long term goals.
2. Hire skilled and talented staff.
3. Identify and understand the developmental needs of your employees.
4. Ensure that all key employees understand their career paths and the roles they are being developed to fill.
5. Focus resources on key employee retention.
6. Be aware of employment trends in your industry to know which roles would be difficult to fill externally.

The Succession Planning Process

Again, some may feel succession planning is only for CEOs. But every key position needs a Succession Plan. One of my colleagues once told me, 'If you become indispensable, surely there's no chance of you being promoted.' He was right. If a person is to be promoted, a trained person has to be ready to take over the position he/she vacates. To effectively implement a succession plan, you need to consider the following:
1. The long-term direction of the company.
2. Key roles and positions which require development of people.

3. Skilled talent whom you want to develop for the future.

4. Company Strategy – Is your succession planning helping you in areas where the returns are the highest?

5. Your Succession Plan has to be dynamic. To be effective, it should be tailored to individual abilities, talents, capabilities and needs of your people.

6. Make a proactive plan (train and develop people before they are needed) rather than a reactive one (looking for an appropriate candidate at the last minute).

Strategy for Succession Planning

To begin with, we need to understand that one size doesn't fit all. How a company approaches its succession planning depends on various things like:

1. The culture and processes of the company

2. The structure and operations of the company

3. The individual capabilities, competencies of the people you wish to groom

4. Capabilities and strengths of the key people (currently doing the key role) and what are they being groomed for

You may not have a Succession Plan for each position, but it is a must for all key positions. It would be necessary to make sure all such key positions are identified at least once a year, advisably more often.

Advantages of Succession Planning

• It ensures a continuous supply of well trained, motivated and involved employees who can readily take over key positions when the need arises. This ensures the future needs of the company are taken care of.

• Not just capable, these people are also well entrenched into the company's culture.

• Helps retain talented and skilled employees by defining

The 3 'T's:

their career paths.
• Enhances the reputation of the organization as a challenging, stimulating place to work, which in turn attracts better talent.
• It acts as the best motivating and engaging factor for an employee.

Succession Planning Pitfalls

1. Lack of a formal written plan for each key person or position.
2. A rigid, inflexible plan NOT tailored to the needs and abilities of the personnel involved.
3. Uncertainty about how long one needs to wait for a promotion may result in the best people leaving.
4. People selected in the succession planning process may not be motivated enough and may have plans of their own.

Points to Ponder

• There is no standard Succession Planning path for companies or individuals. Each situation should be analyzed and optimized in terms of the company's and individual's needs.
• Allow enough time to groom the successors.
• Designate the successor and potential back-ups early on. This will help clarify communication with individuals involved and eliminate disappointment and possible departures of key candidates who may be unaware of this process.

Quality of the individuals selected is vital for successful Succession Planning.

Talent Retention

Retention of key and skilled talent is a critical factor through which a company can maintain its competitive advantage and sustain growth because:

a) Turnover costs (cost of talent replacement, opportunity costs for vacant positions - lost time and productivity and lost business performance) are very high.

b). Skilled performers drive the business performance of a company.

As per the opinion of senior managers in McKinsey's 'War for Talent' study, in an Operations role, high performers can increase productivity by 40%, in Management roles they can increase profits by 49%, and, in Sales positions they can achieve greater revenues by 67%.

Retention Strategies

Talent management strategies directly address the need to retain talent, control costs and increase productivity. While each company may have a portfolio of retention strategies, like compensation packages and rewards, benefits, telecommuting options, work/life balance initiatives, investing to help employees learn and grow etc., managements need to figure out which practices will work in their organizational context and what they should focus on.

Retention Recipes:

a) Recruit Right

• Ensure an accurate match between the role and candidate.
• Automated skills-based matching
• Aim at recruitment of top candidates
• Automate workflow of recruitment process
• Proactively build talent pools of suitable candidates
• Build and mine talent pool database
• Ensure new hires are productive as soon as possible
• Coordinate all on boarding activities

The 3 'T's':

b) Improve Line Management Capability

Once hired, the majority of the responsibility for talent retention shifts to the manager. It is the manager's role to direct, guide, and evaluate the employee. To best equip managers for their job, the correlating talent management practices should be embedded in their everyday business management practices. Hence, managers need visibility into corporate goals and their alignment with tasks and projects along with both past and expected employee performance in order to effectively manage in a dynamic business environment.

c) Manager Excellence

• Manage people based on facts and data
• Single system for all aspects of talent management
• Provide intuitive, useful talent management systems designed for the line manager
• Provide relevant data to support decision-making. [5]

Stay Interviews

A Stay Interview is a preventive tool in employee retention strategy. A stay interview can tell you how the organization can improve and how you can retain your employees. Your employees tell you what you are doing right. A stay interview can build trust with employees and you can assess the degree of employee satisfaction and engagement. Stay interviews provide a two-way conversation, a chance to ask questions and follow-up on ideas.

Monetary and Non-monetary ways of retention:

1) Monetary Methods – Apart from the regular methods like bonuses, rewards, stock options etc. organizations can come up with innovative monetary methods to retain talent. For example, a shipping company has a novel way of retaining top

talent. It signs a new contract with its employees every four months. Every four months, employees can avail leave and come back and sign a new contract. However, there is a threat of the skilled employees not renewing their contracts and taking up employment elsewhere. In order to curb this problem, the company announced that it would increase the pay of the top employees each time they signed a new contract. This policy went a long way in helping them retain experienced talent.

2) Non-monetary Methods – These would comprise of work-from-home opportunities, birthday offs, on-site gymnasiums/exercise classes or reimbursement, flexible working hours, child care aid, growth, learning and career opportunities etc.

Another simple way is the care that the organization takes of its employees. As in the case of Kinetic Honda, the company puts in great efforts to look after its employees. For example, their HR manager would personally visit employees who were unwell to ask about their health. They would also arrange for student loans for the children of employees so that they could get a good education. All these efforts go a long way in ensuring employee retention. [6]

> "You can't expect people to be committed, to be loyal to an organization, to be engaged in an organization, [or] to want to stay in an organization if the company doesn't care about them." – David Sirota

In the first chapter, we have understood the concept of Employer Value Proposition - EVP. There is a direct

The 3 'T's:

Source: (6) Innovation on Two Wheels by Arun Firodia.

correlation between EVP and the Talent Management practices of an organization. It is a complete cycle. EVP plays a major role in the kind of talent a company is able to acquire (Talent Acquisition) while talent development and retention strategies of the company will determine whether the company has an attractive Employee Value proposition - EVP or not for employees to contribute and stay with the organization.

■■■

Caselet

The Challenge of the Decade: The Indian Banking Industry

As per the McKinsey report on the Indian banking structure, 87 percent of General Managers will be superannuated in two years from now (2016-17), leaving a huge gap of those responsible for implementing policy. Also Latha Venkatesh, Banking Editor CNBC TV 18 mentioned in an interview that many private banks are run on/by people poached from the public sector bank(PSB). So, PSBs need to acknowledge that these are national assets and they need to retain the value that they create.

As per the "Indian Banking 2020" report by Boston Consulting Group, FICCI and IBA - The public sector banks enter the next decade with the same expectations as their private sector peers but with a severe disadvantage in human resources. The HR challenge of public sector banks has reached a tipping point. Due to a legacy of several decades, the public sector banks will witness unprecedented loss of skills and competencies in the form of retiring senior and middle management executives over the next few years. That coupled with the need for large scale re–skilling, attracting and retaining fresh talent, controlling the growing employee costs, and introduction of performance discipline are significant challenges.

Public Sector banks will face the following challenges-
1. Demographic Challenge: Almost 80% of the middle management and 50% of the junior–most officers will be lost through retirement within the next 10 years. Crucial competent talent will be lost. There will be a typical

generation gap through new generation recruitment in banks. This emerging manpower profile will leave a generation gap between the young cohort of new hires and the experienced employees to whom they would report. Such a gap creates a disconnect that threatens to damage the assimilation and retention of the new recruits.

2. Attracting Talent and Induction: The public sector banks have to induct new talent and retain them. As PSB employees have been paid very poorly as compared to private banks, attracting talent will be a much bigger challenge.

3. Performance Discipline. Also, the productivity of private sector bank employees is higher than that of public sector bank employees. So the challenge for PSBs is just not to induct new talent and but need to contain staff costs by improving productivity. Improving employee performance will be a challenge.

4. Unlearning: It mentions the need to learn new practices while "unlearning" long–standing practices that are no longer best practices. Re-skilling the staff with new trends and practices will be a bigger challenge.

While PSBs are facing the above challenges, private banks are also taking various steps to retain talent. Private banks are paying higher compensations packages to employees to retain talent and poaching the talent from public sector banks by paying attractive compensation packages. Private Banks are retaining talent by providing employees a combination of bonuses, variable pay and ESOPs and also offering better job profiles and secure career paths. Private banks are identifying their key talent and retaining them by providing large roles and retention pay.

What you need to work on:
1. What are the HR practices that public sector banks should adopt for talent acquisition?
2. How are Private Banks trying to retain talent?
3. In view of above challenges, how should HR practices be transformed in PSBs for talent development and management?

References-
1. "Indian Banking 2020" A report by Boston Consulting Group, FICCI and IBA
2. http://www.governancenow.com/news/regular-story/80-brass-set-retire-psu-banks-look-dry-days
3. http://www.moneycontrol.com/news/business/retain-psu-bank-talent-or-face-national-calamity-rbi-rajan_1062854.html

The 3 'T's:

3

All about Competencies

We are Human…
We work with machines but the driving force
is Human Beings…

The competencies of Human Resources is therefore the key component in organizational success!

An organization is successful when its people put their skills to the best possible use – that is, when its people are competent.

An oft-used concept in HR, competency means the essential understanding, knowledge, aptitude, behavior and proficiency that one needs to successfully perform a job. Competencies could be general i.e. cognitive and social capabilities like problem solving or interpersonal skills, or they could be technical - referring to the specific knowledge and skills required for a job.

To give you an example, innovative ability/creativity as a competency would mean that the employee thinks out of the box, generates hitherto untested ideas, works to improve systems and procedures, encourages innovation etc. If interpersonal skills are his/her competency, they would mean he/she has good relations with colleagues (peers, superiors, subordinates and also people external to the organization) and can instill confidence, trust and goodwill in them for the role he/she performs.

Defining Job Competencies:
If you take an example of a sales team, you will find that job competencies would differ at the level of a sales executive and a team leader. A sales executive needs to be ambitious, a go-getter, good at interactions, networking, determined and so on.

All about Competencies

Just one step higher is the team leader who, apart from all the above, also needs to be a people's person and handle a team of poor, average, good and excellent performers. So while a team leader is capable of doing a sales executive's job, a sales executive may not have the competence to do the team leader's job just yet. This competency can be developed in the Sales Executive over time.

In order to have the right person for the right job, an organization (or you as the HR Manager) needs to define the competencies required for each position. In order to align training and development such that it results into highly skilled manpower, organizations today are trying to define key competencies across roles.

Defining competencies will help:
1. An organization to define what its employees 'must do' to produce desired results.
2. Employees to clearly comprehend what they require to be 'productive'.
3. Organizations to assess their employees' skills, attitude and behavior and their lacunae.
4. Skill gaps to be identified and deploying the resources/inputs needed for employees to acquire/develop those competencies.
5. You would have understood now, that competency identification is a crucial job for the leader. Each person is unique and has different competencies. The leader should have a complete SWOT analysis of each member of his team to perform any critical tasks. Such tasks would require different permutations and combinations of employee competencies for the final output. For this, a structured method is required to handle the talent of a team. This is called Competency Mapping.

Competencies present a whole-person approach to individual assessment.

What is the scope of Competency Mapping?

Each person is a combination of certain strengths and weaknesses. To be successful, an organization needs to capitalize on the strengths of their employees such that they can be utilized to the maximum and their weaknesses can be overcome.

Competency Mapping means evaluating/identifying an employee's/organization's strengths, weaknesses and job skills of its existing employees. An HR Manager has a key role to play here.

> There is a special element (shine/glow) in each employee. An HR manager works like a jeweller. Not only can he/she accurately spot a diamond within the employees, he/she can also spot the special element in each employee that makes him/her a gem for the organization.

Competency Mapping will help you understand how best to use each employee's strengths or combine the strengths of different employees, so that they can overcome each other's weaknesses to produce the highest quality output. You may have heard the story of the blind man and the lame man. Due to their handicaps, they could go nowhere by themselves. But when they came together, the blind man walked, carrying his lame friend on his shoulders and as the lame man could see, he guided the blind man. This is a classic example of team work and combining the strengths of people.

In a closer to home context, this is exactly what Bhuvan

All about Competencies

(Aamir Khan) does in the super hit Bollywood film 'Lagaan'. To build a winning cricket team with people who had never played cricket before, he first identified the competencies he would need in a team, namely, players who could run like the wind, had immense stamina, had strong arms to hit the ball with great force etc. He carefully chose each team member based on his competencies. He even chose an outcast, crippled man for his ability to spin the ball with his crippled hand. He cast these team members in roles (batting, bowling, fielding etc.) as per their competencies and encouraged them to hone their skills to perfection, leading them on to a surprising victory against the mighty English Cricket Team.

At the individual level, Competency Mapping helps employees answer the question – 'What is my core strength?' It helps employees plan and prepare for a career change or advancement. Most Competency Mapping models bifurcate strengths into functional and behavioral skills.

Functional means those skills needed to actually perform the job. These are measurable and can indicate whether people can really do the job! What would the functional requirements for an accountant be? We can put down many like being a commerce graduate, being computer literate, the ability to operate accountancy software, good record keeping etc.

Behavioral skills are soft skills which are hard to measure. How would you measure skills like good communication, language proficiency, networking skills, team spirit etc.? To analyze them, you as an HR manager need to design questions and tests that accurately identify behavioral strengths and weaknesses. You might want to focus on how the person sets his goals or adapts to changes, deals with failure etc. This type of testing is important to get a complete picture of an individual's skill-sets.

Steps for Competency Mapping :

1. First, conduct a Job Analysis. Design a questionnaire and get a relevant set of employees (sample) to fill it up. The idea is to understand what they feel are the key behaviors required to perform their jobs.

⬇

2. Based on the Job Analysis and the responses of the questionnaires, develop a Competency-based Job Description.

⬇

3. Use the competency-based Job Description to map competencies. The competencies derived become the basis for assessing performance.

⬇

4. Through performance assessment, identify areas where training is needed and competencies which need to be developed.

How do companies map competencies?
Competency Mapping is generally undertaken through various methods like Assessment Centre, Critical Incident's Technique, Interview Simulations/Role plays, Questionnaires, Group Discussions, Psychometric Tests, Case Study Analysis, etc. The process begins by identifying competencies that are most important for a specific position. For instance, if the post of a manager is to be filled internally, the hiring manager needs to list the required job skills and ideal behavioral traits needed for the position. From this list,

a questionnaire mapping each candidate's competencies in the desired areas can be made. After all the candidates answer the questionnaire, the hiring manager along with HR can then compare the results using the competency scores to determine the best person for the promotion.

Of course, for this, carefully worded questions, very specific to the job are required to eliminate vague answers. Don't ask ambiguous questions like, "How good are you at Time Management?" The answer to this will always be relative. Instead, try a question like, "How many projects have you finished before your deadlines?" Not only is the reply to this question objective, but it can also be verified.

Benefits of Competency Mapping -
A. For the Organization:
1. It helps improve employee performance,
2. Helps with the hiring or promotion decisions and
3.Provides a critical and analytical look at the current workforce.

B. For Individuals:
Competency Mapping for Individuals is like looking at your own face in the mirror and understanding your best features. If one knows that problem solving and communication skills are one's strength, those can be emphasized upon in an interview. A company which is looking for these skills will value such an employee over others.

While all of us may be fully competent in 3-4 areas, our proficiency may be low in a few others. Competency mapping will help us realize and emphasize on the areas which we want to develop. It can give clear pointers to prepare action plans required to cultivate those competencies. Accordingly, we realize how far we need to go or we need to change the kind of work we do/culture we work in to perform well.

Challenges of Competency Mapping–
A. For Organizations:

1. The Process: The organization needs to be committed to and ready to put in the required time and efforts required for the process of Competency Mapping. If enough time is not given, the results may not be very useful. Some companies choose to hire an external consulting team to handle the modeling, testing & analysis process for them.

2. Implementation: Of course, there is no point in coming up with results of competency mapping if they are not going to be implemented. This might result in changes in Job Descriptions, change of responsibilities or splitting or merging of departments. Training and incentive programs may also be needed. Usually, people are insecure and may hesitate to accept the clear picture in the mirror, and accept the changes and training required, but this is the challenge. An HR manager has to perform this task smoothly for improved productivity and better employee morale.

B. For Individuals:

You will be surprised to find that many people have many assumptions about themselves. They may feel that they are not very good at "X" but are the best at "Y". Competency Mapping may end up shattering their beliefs and in turn their sentiments. So, in order to retain its utility and acceptance of results , the people taking the test need to do so with an open mind.

All about Competencies

Competency Assessment:

> "If you think you can do it, that's
> Confidence; if you do it that's Competence."
> - Morris Code.

The comprehensive list of specific job skills required for the job, which are derived from Competency Mapping forms the basis of a Competency Assessment. It is one of the core elements of Talent Management. Competency Assessment compares employee performance on two parameters - the necessary job skills and the set performance standards.

The key to Competency Assessment is to assess people as they use their knowledge and skills on the job. It provides a method of building the knowledge and skills needed by employees to perform their present jobs. We have seen Succession Planning in Talent Management (Refer Chapter 2). Competency Assessment is a key element of the Succession Planning process since it provides a way of developing employees for their future roles.

Process of Competency Assessment:

There are many different ways of assessing competencies. The well-known method below provides an objective assessment and better quality outcomes.

[1]

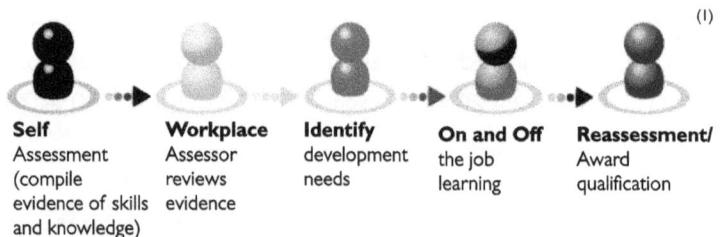

Self Assessment (compile evidence of skills and knowledge)

Workplace Assessor reviews evidence

Identify development needs

On and Off the job learning

Reassessment/ Award qualification

Source: (1) http://www.cognology.com.au/learning_center/cbawhatis/

1. The process begins with self-assessment by the employees against a set of competencies. They compile evidence which shows that they are competent.

2. A workplace assessor reviews the evidence and verifies the performance.

3. Development needs are identified.

4. The employee uses both "on-the-job" and "off-the-job" learning to develop the areas identified.

5. After a specific period, the employee is reassessed and if he/she can demonstrate the skills, they are assessed as "competent".

Competency Assessment
A. For Organizations:
• Helps raise employee productivity by empowering them with the capacity to meet their objectives. This is turn increases organization profitability.

• Plays a very important role in Succession Planning.

• It is an objective method of assessment

• Identifies areas where employees need training which can be carried out "on-the-job".

•To execute a project, an organization can put together teams of people with complementary skills.

B. For Employees:
• It is an objective method of assessment for employees.

•The employee can learn at his/her own speed and "on-the-job".

• It takes into account existing skills.

•An employee can acquire skills that will help him/her in the current as well as future roles.

Benefits of Competency Assessments:
Competency Assessment is a continuous process that is

undertaken in Corporates in order to track the developments and improvements in skills in an employee's competencies over a period of time.

Competency Assessments work as skill checklists which employees and employers can keep over time to note employee performance. They help to create a benchmark for measuring performance vis-à-vis standards in the organization, work as a tool for assessing performance, recognize and reward satisfactory performance, highlight shortfalls in performance, bring less proficient areas to light in order to identify training needs, help to provide continuous coaching for employees and establish standards of competence in the organization.

Organizations are not only about achieving profits. They are a source for the fulfillment of the ambitions, aspirations and dreams of their employees. Enhancing Employee Competence is what can turn these dreams into reality!

■ ■ ■

Caselet

'Developing' a Competency Model @ JiBABA

JiBABA, a global e-commerce company wanted to create a formal development path for succession into key management positions in the organization. The HR team was finding it difficult to find suitably qualified and interested candidates internally. Since the company was growing rapidly in the global scenario, the HR team faced the following challenges:

• Listing the required skills and major responsibilities for each role and clearly communicating its scope.

• Attracting candidates for senior internal positions.

• Creating consistency in the position and role requirement across various countries and business units.

• Defining a complete set of e-commerce competencies within a few months.

The HR team undertook the following steps by consulting Industrial and Organizational Psychology experts.

1. Collection of data: To integrate the global management structure and achieve maximum buy-in for the process, the HR team gathered critical job information - both, Technical skills and Behavioral traits in three different ways:

• In-person focus groups
• Web-based focus groups
• One-on-one telephone interviews

Using these three formats provided flexibility and expedited the data collection process. The HR team got important first-hand details from the employees. For all of the roles, the HR

All about Competencies

team also collected job information from the incumbent's manager to ensure that all current (as well as future) skills were taken into account.

2. Conversion of behaviors into competencies: Qualitative data was used to design a customized competency model for the management positions. The competency model needed to highlight areas of particular importance to the organization due to distinctive organization culture. The competencies related to behaviours addressing constant change and uncertainty, vital trends of the industry, monitoring competition and other behaviours not commonly found in a standard competency model were included.

3. Content validity: After developing the competency model, it was required to be tested within the current management population to ensure its relevance and usefulness. After the draft version of the competency model was developed, this was presented to the industry experts hired by the company in order to gather more feedback on specific wording and terminology. It was also provided to the HR Team and Department managers so that they could use them in a mock assessment with staff members and determine whether the behaviors defined in the model were appropriate. The model was also presented to the Board of Directors for final review.

The above competency modeling helped to identify the unique technical skills and behavioral qualities (competencies) required for the key positions for the success of JiBABA in an evolving industry. The HR team first used this competency model for measuring the performance of current managers and developing a suitable training plan and program to train potential current managers for future key positions.

After a years' time, when JiBABA's HR team implemented the entire competency model, it helped high-potential candidates to more clearly understand the skills needed and scope of these key leadership positions. The HR team could make a more defined career path for these managers. The model helped the company to define consistent standards and expectations for various roles across business units and countries.

The structured competency model also helped to attract the best candidates from within for these challenging positions. Learning opportunities could be provided so that employees could excel in their career growth within the company.

What you need to work on:
1. Was it really necessary for JiBABA to do competency mapping? Justify.
2. How did the JiBABA team develop the competency model for key management positions?
3. What benefits could be derived by developing the Competency Model?

All about Competencies

4
Compensation & Benefits

Long ago when I was still a young executive, out of curiosity my boss asked me what my thoughts on Compensation were.

I answered, "Firstly, compensation should be such that it allows an employee to 'Spend a little, Save a little and Stretch a little'. Secondly, compensation should increase in direct proportion to the employee's contribution."

She asked me to elaborate and I said, "Compensation should be such that the employee can fulfill his/her basic necessities, put aside a little for the future and yet work towards earning more. While the fulfilling of necessities and savings would keep him/her satisfied, the need for more would encourage better performance in order to earn more benefits, better incentives, a promotion etc". But for this to work, it is necessary for compensation to be in direct proportion to an employee's contribution.

> Good compensation and benefits add to the Employer Value Proposition of an organization. There is a direct correlation between Compensation and Benefits offered to the employees and Talent Acquisition & Retention.

Defining Compensation
An employee contributes to the organization's growth by utilizing his/her skills and time. Compensation includes not only salary, but also direct & indirect rewards & benefits given by the organization to an employee for his/her contribution. It is a tool used by the organization to foster the values, culture and behavior they require. It is an instrument that enables the organization to achieve its business objectives.

Compensation & Benefits

Types of Compensation

Financial

Non - Financial

Growth and Development
Opportunities, Training
and Development
Opportunities,
Career Development,
Recognition, Healthy
Work Environment

Direct Financial Compensation

Paid at regular intervals
Salaries/Wages, Bonus
Incentives/Commissions

Indirect Financial Compensation

Other benefits like
retirement plans, leaves,
Benefits, Employee services

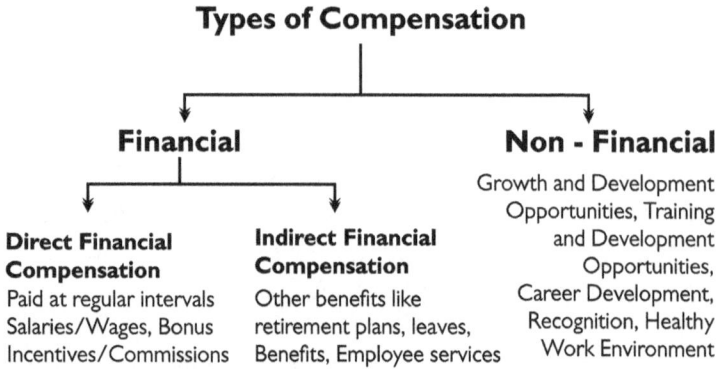

Determining Compensation

> While determining compensation, organizations should remember that their best investment is their people. Their results are directly proportionate to their investment in people.

Ideally, organizations should develop a compensation and rewards program outlining an equitable process for compensation. A combination of wages, benefits and rewards in the right balance will ensure a competitive edge today and a sustainable strategy for tomorrow. You, as an HR manager will have to determine compensation in the following situations:

• New appointments
• Existing employees due for a raise (annual increment)
• An employee taking up a new role
• Valuable talent which may be prone to leaving due to compensation
• Market conditions
• Critical/scarce skills or expertise

While determining compensation, ensure that the approach you take is guided by your organization's compensation philosophy and is applied consistently. Make sure that established principles/guidelines are followed. This will help you maintain the critical balance between organizational needs and the individual considerations to arrive at an optimal compensation structure.

How to determine Base Pay – Approaches and Techniques

Base pay is a fixed regular payment made to an employee in exchange for performance of the duties and responsibilities of his/her role.

$$Base\ Pay = Basic + Allowances$$

How you determine the base pay is totally dependent on your compensation philosophy. Remember that your approach should result in your organization maintaining its competitiveness in the market on the one hand and retaining its consistency and credibility on the other. To determine base pay, an HR manager needs to factor in the following:
1. The role of the position in the organization
2. Complexity of tasks & responsibilities
3. Market and sector-wise data.

Pay Increases

Pay increases happen when an increase is made in the base pay. There are various reasons and methods for determining an increase.

Cost of living increase

This is an increase offered to account for increases in the cost of living. It is offered regardless of performance, with the intention of increasing the base pay for each role on the

Compensation & Benefits

salary scale by a set percentage. These increases are generally done on an annual basis, and are given to all existing employees. It is dependent on the overall financial stability of the organization. The new trend among small organizations is to move away from offering a cost of living increase and perform market adjustments instead.

Market adjustment after reviewing compensation against pre-established criteria

Market adjustments are made based on market survey data on compensation. This data is usually received and evaluated towards the end of either the fiscal or calendar year. Organizations evaluate salaries against market data and adjust base salaries for roles that are below the market data. On the contrary, if a position is overpaid as compared to the market data, some companies notify the employees of this and do not provide them an increase. Here, the employees are considered to be 'red circled' (unable to qualify for salary increases until their salary comes in line with market).

Promotional increase

A promotion is the advancement of an employee to a higher level of responsibility than his/her current position. Promotions are generally based on performance and availability of opportunities. Generally, promotions are announced once a year after performance appraisals.

Merit increase

As the name suggests, Merit increases recognize an employee's contribution and compensate them for a high level of performance. Performance is the key factor in awarding a merit increase.

Bonus payments

A Bonus is paid over and above the specified wages or salary and is only distributed as the organization is able to pay or as per the employment contract. It helps improve employee motivation, morale and productivity or may be paid as recognition to employees achieving a significant goal.

In most companies, employees (who have completed more than a year with the organization) are paid a bonus at the end of the Performance Assessment Year. For blue collared workmen, typically bonus is paid in the festival month (Diwali / Durga Pooja).

Incentive plans

They reward employees for improved commitment and performance and as a means of motivation. They are designed to supplement base pay and fringe benefits. Financial incentive plans may offer a percentage of base salary or a cash bonus. Non-financial incentive plans offer non-monetary benefits such as additional paid vacations or increased professional development (education sponsorship etc.)

Communication

The need for effectively communicating with employees about their compensation cannot be over emphasized. Employees who understand their compensation plan and its value can be sure that they are being compensated fairly which results in greater motivation & retention (cost to company-CTC).

The crux of this communication is making them aware of the 'value' of their compensation plan. The strategy for communicating with the employees regarding compensation must be aligned with the organization's HR strategy and must have the support of the management.

A high level of transparency, though a plus, would actually depend on the organization's culture. The communication should advise employees about their salaries, job grade/level, where their salary stands in the salary range for their respective job grade/level, the basis for progress through seniority or performance, and annual salary adjustments (if any).

A variety of formats can be used for the communication. Printed material like statements, booklets, letters, newsletters and memos allow employees to refer to the material later. Face-to-face interaction through meetings, workshops and ongoing support allows individual questions and concerns to be addressed immediately. Remember, it is vital to ensure that your employees have access to information regarding their compensation plans/structure and that it is provided to them in a clear and concise language. Apart from internal use, communicating the compensation plan externally can help attract prospective employees (eg. Pre-placement talks in Engineering / Management institutes).

Advantages of Compensation & Benefits:
1. Employer Value Proposition: A well designed compensation and benefits strategy adds value to the Employer Value Proposition helping to attract, motivate and retain talent. This will also lead to addition in the Employee Value Proposition whereby the employee will add better value to the organization through his/her work.

2. Job satisfaction: If your employees are satisfied, they would love to work for you and put in that extra bit whenever

required.

3. Motivation: We are all motivated by the fulfillment of our needs. A compensation plan that addresses employee needs shall motivate them towards desired results contributing to long term employee engagement.

4. Low Absenteeism: If employees love what they do and are satisfied with the compensation, there is bound to be low absenteeism.

5. Low Turnover: Needless to say, compensation and benefits based on sound principles are one of the best retention strategies an organization could have.

6. Peace of Mind: Your compensation and benefits plan works as an assurance to employees and relieves them of insecurity, so that they can work with peace of mind and achieve their goals.

7. Increases self-confidence: A good compensation and benefits plan boosts the confidence of the employee and ingrains a can-do attitude in him/her.

Rewarding Employees

Swati's company was looking for an anchor for a one-day event. When they couldn't find one, she gladly volunteered and did a fine job. Her boss immediately announced a cash reward for her. She was shocked and disappointed. She felt that a simple word of appreciation would have been enough. The cash reward made her feel that the management thought she had volunteered with the expectation of a reward.

Suhas, a loyal employee with a software company was

surprised when his 10-year service award package offered him cash. Though he could do with the little extra money, the fact that his employer had put a price tag on ten years of his life left him feeling hurt.

> You must realize that for an employee, a Reward is an Honor. The feeling of honoring an employee must reflect in the HR policy. How an employee is rewarded and the way this is communicated to him/her goes a long way in determining his/her perception of the reward.

While it is a common perception that employees would like to be rewarded in cash or are most motivated by money, research shows that it's the least effective form of recognition. Why do employees feel confused, offended or even hurt when cash or money is given in the form of rewards?

The answer is, it's like asking a friend what he/she wants for their birthday! It implies that you don't know and are buying a gift more out of obligation than desire. The same goes for employees. If they even get a tiny hint that you're attempting to manipulate them with a monetary reward, it will make them emotionally disengaged and they may feel insulted.

You must realize that for an employee, a Reward is an Honor. The honor must be reflected in the reward given to the employee and in the HR policy as well. How an employee is rewarded and the way this is communicated to him/her goes a long way in determining his/her perception of the reward.

The example of Kirloskar Oil Engines is this regard is a brilliant one. They have a superb reward policy for employees above the middle management level i.e. AGM, GM, VP and above. On the day of announcing these rewards, they are told that apart from the regular benefits given to them, they will be given a bigger surprise at the end of the day. This creates a curiosity in the employee's mind.

As he/she leaves for the day, he/she is handed over a key. The key belongs to a black car which is the company's gift to the employee. The employee is completely bowled over. As per protocol, all senior employees of the company have cars which are black in color. This is also an attempt at maintaining equity among these employees. Gifting an employee a car, not just of any color but a black one is telling the employee that he/she has arrived! He/she is now a part of the special, treasured senior management. Such minute thought has gone into the designing of this company's rewards.

Any guesses what effect this would have had on the Employer Value Proposition of this company?

Recognition is a powerful management tool and must be used well for the organization's and employee's benefit. It is only through honest emotional engagement that your financial/non-financial rewards will help you to create a measurable, bankable ROI.

Here, I would like to recommend the Four Cornerstone Approach by John Schaefer:

1. **Communication:** People need to know how to give recognition, rather than just presenting awards;

2. Training: This focuses on the "how to do" and is important for overall performance improvement. Effective training on how to give recognition avoids your best intentions from being seen as nothing more than "throwing 'em a bone";

3. Reinforcement: Recognition is not an event, it's a process. Employees must "want to" achieve business goals, but how can this emotional engagement be achieved? It can be done by validating. Employees must feel important and appreciated when they go the extra mile;

4. Measurements: You must have heard the famous saying "What gets measured, gets done". Things that are measured tend to improve. Measurements highlight performance. Good performance needs to be recognized.[1]

The right manner of recognition presents an opportunity to turn budgeted expenses into profits. It is an excellent method of employee engagement which can result in improved productivity, profitability, enhanced morale and teamwork, along with significant reductions in turnover, recruiting and safety related costs.

Performance Management System (PMS)
It is a process which contributes to the effective management of talent (individuals and teams) in order to achieve improved levels of employee and organizational performance and development.

Why Performance Management System?
As we saw, Talent Management is a continuous process to achieve the strategic goal of the organization. While Talent Management is about harnessing the skills and knowledge of the available talent, Performance Management is a process of

Source: (1) www.schaeferrecognitiongroup.com

monitoring, measuring and evaluating performance against strategic goals.

Guidelines for Developing a Performance Management System
Performance management goes way beyond just doing an annual review for an employee. It is about continuously working together with that employee, identifying his/her strengths and development areas and helping him/her to become a more productive and effective worker. An HR manager must know how to develop/effectively implement a performance management system in order to be in a position to help everyone in the organization work to their full potential.

1. Begin by assessing the performance appraisal process that is currently in place. Analyze the type of feedback the employees are getting through this process. Is there a need to change or make additions to the evaluation process? Or would it be enough to build on what you already have, or is there a need to develop a new system altogether?

2. Identify organizational goals clearly. A Performance Management System should be designed to help employees achieve organizational goals - so take a good look at what these goals are. In this process of identifying goals, it would make sense to freeze on your sales goals as well as the new products/services that you would like to develop. Identify processes or procedures that could be simplified or done more effectively. Share your expectation for better communication between departments and staff members.

3. Clearly communicate the organization's expectation to each employee. Acknowledge their performance. This will

encourage them. You also need to share "areas for improvement" and how to improve them. Point out specific goals which you would like them to accomplish. Prioritize these so the employee is aware of what is topmost on the list and the deadline for each goal. Then comes the task of monitoring their performance throughout the year. If they appear to be struggling to meet performance goals, speak to them to understand what the problem is and if they require support or coaching.

4. Evaluate performance. During each periodic formal performance review, let employees know how they are doing. Provide specific feedback on their performance. Let them know where they stand. Let them also know where superlative performance will lead them to and the penalties of underperformance. Find out, if any grievances or problems need to be addressed.

Typically in organizations, formal performance reviews happen twice a year – Mid-year review & Annual review (year-end). However, depending on the role and need of the job holder – informal reviews can be done more often as an ongoing process.

Checklist for People managers –
• Ensure employees have clearly defined goals and objectives
• Provide candid feedback on individual performance
• Specify the period for the objectives to be achieved
• Define the right attitude, knowledge and skills for effective individual performance
• Determine a training, education and development plan for the employee
•Undertake timely evaluation and fair assessment of employee's performance

• Identify deficits through performance management, bring them to the attention of the employee, and address them through training and workplace support; and

• Document all interactions with the employee during performance reviews.

The Performance Management Cycle

There is much more to performance management than the annual performance review meeting.

Performance management is a continuous process of three phases:[2]

1.   Planning,
2.   Monitoring and
3.   Reviewing employee performance.

Let's understand what happens in each phase.

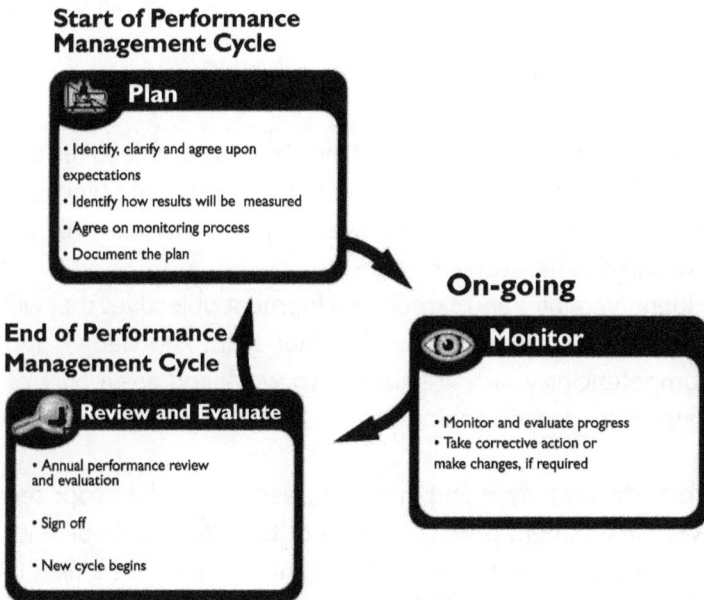

Start of Performance Management Cycle

Plan
• Identify, clarify and agree upon expectations
• Identify how results will be measured
• Agree on monitoring process
• Document the plan

On-going

Monitor
• Monitor and evaluate progress
• Take corrective action or make changes, if required

End of Performance Management Cycle

Review and Evaluate
• Annual performance review and evaluation
• Sign off
• New cycle begins

Compensation & Benefits

Source: (2)http://hrcouncil.ca/hr-toolkit/keeping-people-performance-management.cfm

Phase I - Planning

The first phase is a combined effort involving both managers and employees. In this phase they:

• Review that particular employee's Job Description to determine if it reflects the work that the employee is currently doing. In case of new/additional responsibilities or job change, the job description is updated.

• Once the Job description is finalized, the employee's work plan is reviewed to check if it takes him/her to the achievement of the organization's goals and objectives.

• A work plan comprising of deliverables, expected results along with timelines to evaluate performance is finalized.

• Next, between three to five areas will be identified which will be the key objectives (Goal sheet / Key Performance Indicators - KPI's) for the employee to achieve that year. These areas will be determined by

a. The organization's strategic plan,

b. The employee's aspirations to better performance in a particular area, or

c. The need to highlight a particular aspect of the job at a particular time.

The employee should understand that these objectives are critical for his/her overall success. If these critical objectives are not fulfilled, his/her overall performance will be evaluated as unsatisfactory.

• Identify training and career development objectives that will help the employee improve his/ her skills, knowledge, and competencies which are related to work and are a part of long-term career planning.

Both, the employee and manager need to sign the proposed work assessment plan. One copy of the plan should be with the employee for his records and another should be filed in his/her personnel file/folder.

Setting objectives and measurements

Managers need to ensure that the performance objectives and measures or indicators of success are representative of the full range of duties carried out by the employee, especially those everyday tasks that take time to complete but are often overlooked as insignificant accomplishments.

Most Performance Management Systems have weightages (%) allocated to each goal and an overall rating scale for final evaluation.

It is a commonly known fact that objectives should be SMART i.e.

Specific
Specify clearly What, When, Who and How much is to be accomplished.

Measurable
Objectives need to be measurable so that they answer the questions: How much? How many? How will I know when it is accomplished? Multiple measures should be used if possible, for example, quantity, quality, time frame and cost.

Attainable
Assure yourself that objectives are attainable.

Realistic
The level of complexity of the objective should match the employee's skills, experience and capability.

Time-bound
Be clear about the time frame in which performance objectives are to be achieved.

Compensation & Benefits

Phase 2 - Monitoring

It is not enough to just draw up plans. Monitoring day-to-day performance means managers must focus attention on results achieved by employees, individual behaviors and team dynamics. Regular meetings of the employee with the manager should take place to:
• Evaluate progress towards objectives
• Identify barriers and troubleshooting
• Share feedback on progress
• Identify changes required to the work plan to factor in change in the organization priorities or new responsibilities of the employee
• Determine whether extra support or guidance is to be given to the employee

Continuous coaching

Coaching is a requirement of Performance management as it addresses concerns and performance related issues. To Coach is to provide direction, guidance, and support wherever required by the employee. In order to coach employees, managers must identify strengths and weaknesses of employees and work with them to leverage their strengths and improve upon the development areas.

Providing feedback

Timely, specific and frequent feedback can make a positive difference to an employee. Positive feedback for good work done will make a big difference to an employee's morale.

Constructive feedback alerts the employee to an area where performance needs to improve. It should be descriptive (give them a specific example) and be directed to the action, not the person. It helps people understand where they stand as compared to expected performance standards.

While positive feedback is easily shared, providing constructive feedback to address a performance issue can be tough. But it's necessary to do this, before it escalates into a bigger problem. Here are a few do's while giving constructive feedback:
1. Have a rational approach during the communication
2. Refrain from getting personal
3. Give them clarity about the agreed goals and the gaps in performance.
4. Patiently listen to the other side of the story.
5. Get them to come up with their solutions.
6. Document the action plan
7. Monitor results periodically. If the issue is not resolved, spell out the consequences/corrective action.

Phase 3 - Reviewing
Performance assessment provides an opportunity to review, summarize and highlight employee performance over the course of the review period.

Self-assessment is an important part of most performance appraisals. Here, an employee uses the performance plan and assessment form as a guide, and assesses his/her own performance prior to the appraisal meeting.

The tasks successfully completed during the last financial year are reviewed against the previous year's goals. Key achievements and shortfalls are identified. Areas of concern and those which require training or coaching are highlighted.

In case, there is disagreement with the feedback shared or rating, the manager needs to resolve it at his level. Else, the

Compensation & Benefits

employee may choose to escalate the same to his N+2(Manager's manager). As an HR manager, you need to be closely involved in the whole process and need to ensure satisfactory resolution of the issue so that no grievances are carried forward into the new Performance cycle.

The assessment form should be signed by both, the employee and the manager. Finally, it becomes part of the employee's personnel file.

Performance Management is a continuous process and after completing the third phase, the organization moves on to a new/next cycle of Performance Management.

Employees are an organization's most strategic resource. They put their heart and soul into the work they do which contributes towards achieving organizational goals. Hence, your compensation and benefits strategy must compensate and reward them to ensure adequate motivation and productivity.

Caselet

Compensation "Matters"

Geeta Sales and Services was into the business of marketing and selling kitchen appliances throughout India. In the South division of Geeta Sales, Mr. Ganeshan was the sole responsible manager managing a team of 100 sales personnel. He conducted sales review meetings every month. He was very friendly and got along with all the sales personnel. He always listened to the managers and accepted their suggestions. The overall contribution of the South Division, helped Geeta Sales to surpass its targets year on year.

In one meeting, one of the sales person – Mr. Bhavesh Shah raised an issue of the uniform compensation system being followed by Geeta Sales. He mentioned that despite achieving the targets, he was not being compensated well as compared to his non-performing team members. The incentives received by all the team members were the same. Bhavesh mentioned that many a times, he had achieved double the sales as compared to his team members but he had not been rewarded for the same. It was de-motivating for Bhavesh as non-performing team members were also getting the same incentives as him. Few of the other team members also expressed concern over the same issue.

Mr. Ganeshan then mentioned that he was unable to solve the problem as it was a management decision and an organizational issue. He shared with the employees that he had suggested to the management to provide performance-based variable pay but they had not considered it. He mentioned that the company had standardized the method of payment which depended on the number of days the employee worked. However, he assured Bhavesh and the other employees that he would once again raise the issue with the top management.

In the next month's meeting, Mr. Ganeshan was not his usual self with the employees as he was told that the management had not accepted his suggestion of performance-based variable pay. On the contrary, Mr. Ganeshan tried to convince the employees that the management was looking into the matter and would come up with a solution soon to resolve the issue. Even after two months, Bhavesh and other good performing team members did not receive any solution to the compensation issue. After that, quite a few good performers from the South Division including Bhavesh left the organization.

Mr. Ganeshan was left mostly with non-performing team members and the performance of the South division of Geeta Sales was dismal as compared to their performance in the last six months. The management questioned Mr. Ganeshan for the non-performance of the South division. At this time, he once again explained the need to introduce the performance-based variable incentive system. Geeta Sales performance was going down in most of its other divisions as well. In the same month, the management asked Mr. Ganeshan to present the plan to introduce a performance-based variable pay system.

What you need to work on:
1. What's was the current compensation system at Geeta Sales? Why did it lead to dissatisfaction among the good performers?

2. Why did Geeta Sales face dismal performance in the South and other divisions too?

3. Why was Mr. Ganeshan insisting on introducing the Performance-based variable pay? How would it help the organization?

4. If you were the HR manager at Geeta Sales, what would be the key factors that you would have in the proposal for the Performance-based variable pay? Would you prepare it on your own or work with Mr. Ganeshan on it?

Compensation & Benefits

5
Organization Development

O + D = OD

What is an Organization (O)?

You must be wondering why I have raised this question here. But instead of going into the why, let's answer it. An organization is a group of individuals and assets which come together for the pursuit of common goals.

What is Development (D)?

It is a process of transformation which leads to progress and improvement.

Now, if we put the two together,

'O + D' = Organization Development (OD).

Every organization has its systems and procedures in place. But that's not enough for a business to run in today's dynamic environment. There is a need to check if these systems and procedures are running effectively and serving the purpose they have been put in place for. Just as important is factoring new developments, improvements and changes (due to market forces) into the organization's process. This means that over time, organizations need to change, evolve, improve and become more effective. This is the process of Organization Development.

Organization development (OD) is a process based on social and behavioral sciences that has the potential to enhance knowledge, skills, proficiency, productivity, satisfaction, income and interpersonal relations for the benefit of a person, team, organization, community, nation, region, or even the entire humanity. OD is an interdisciplinary field which relies on contributions from business, as well as social and behavioral sciences like industrial/organizational psychology, HR, communication and many other disciplines.

OD facilitates efforts made for change. Through OD, an organization can address each issue with due respect to the existing system. Appropriate interventions or changes to individual behavior as well as to the organization's structure, systems, processes and social norms is made after carefully considering the existing systems. While doing so, OD takes into consideration the dynamism of human behavior which is motivated not only by rationality but also by emotional elements, such as sense of pride and belonging.

When is the right time for Organization Development to be implemented?

Today, organizations face a lot of challenges due to an extremely dynamic business environment. In this scenario, the trust level of an employee as well as his/her satisfaction levels need to be maintained on a continuous basis.

Employees' issues and also conflicts need to be taken seriously. Appropriate solutions involving employees must be found so that they also feel that they are a part of the solution. Also, once these problems and issues are resolved, they can concentrate on contributing to the goals of the organization.

An organization will need to apply OD when it wants to
• Develop or improve the organization's mission or vision statement
• Align functional structures in the organization so that they work together to achieve a common goal

• Develop a strategic plan about decision making for the organization's future and its road map
• Make planned improvements
• Manage conflict among individuals, groups, functions, etc. which upsets the harmony of the organization
• Assess the current work environment, identify strengths on which to build and areas in which change and improvement are needed
• Improve current methods, systems, policies and procedures to ensure better running of the organization
• Provide help, support and coaching especially to senior employees to do their jobs better
• Create systems and conduct studies to give individuals feedback on performance and coaching to help them in their individual development.

Core Characteristics of OD
• It is a knowledge-based approach designed to develop values, attitudes, norms, and practices that result in a healthy organizational climate that rewards healthy behavior.
• OD is driven by humanistic values.
• It is aligned to the organization and business objectives.
• Its goal is to improve organizational effectiveness.
• It has a system's orientation and emphasizes a process to achieve results.
• It is an interdisciplinary and behavioral science approach. Varied fields such as organization behavior, management, business, behavioral sciences like psychology, sociology, anthropology, economics, education, counseling, and public administration contribute to OD.
• The change required for OD targets the entire organization, its departments, work groups, employees and may even extend to include a community, nation or region.
• In order to be implemented, OD needs the commitment,

Organization Development

support and involvement of the top management.
• OD needs a meticulous plan. It is a long-term and continuous process for managing change, although it also takes into consideration the ability to respond quickly in today's dynamic situation.
• The process of OD takes place with interventions in the organization's processes and structures and requires skills in working with individuals, groups and the whole organization.
• It is guided by a change agent, change team, or line management whose role is more of a facilitator, teacher, coach and counselor rather than a subject matter expert.
• It recognizes the need for planned follow-up to maintain changes. [1]

Advantages of OD
OD is fast catching up as a popular field due to the value-added concepts and tools that it has introduced to organizations and their various stakeholders like customers, shareholders, employees, management, the community, and even the nation.
1. It establishes an environment supporting creativity, innovation and increased job satisfaction.
2. Develops positive and harmonious interpersonal relationships.
3. Fosters higher employee participation in creating and defining organizational plans and goals.
4. Increases effectiveness and efficiency of the organization which in turn helps it to improve its work environment, provide better-quality products and services, increase profitability, improve share value and support management in its leadership role. [1]

Source: (1)Organization Development: Principles, Processes, Performance by Gary N. McLean, www.bkconnection.com

OD has gained a lot of significance due to complex work issues currently and will be so in future too. No leader has the magic wand to drive change single-handedly. To build a high-performing organization, critical factors are engaged employees and an empowering culture.

Organization Development Process

If OD is so beneficial for an organization, let us understand its process in detail.

It is a cyclical process which begins with an identified problem or need for change and ends when the desired developmental result is obtained.

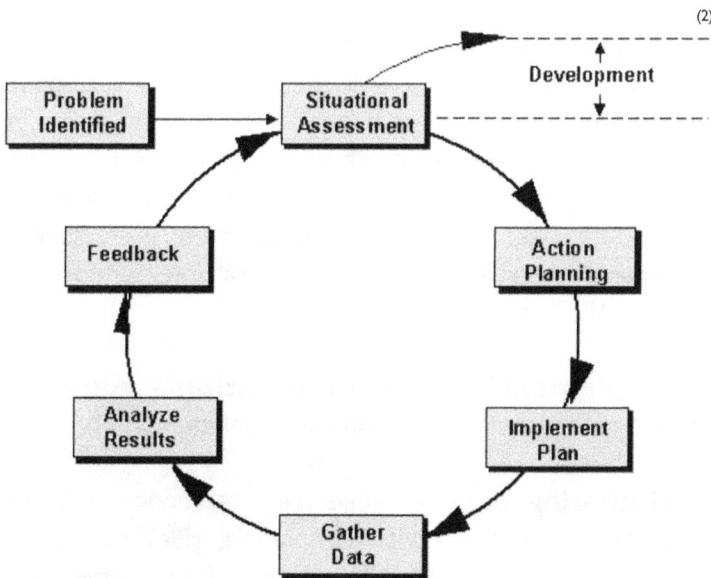

1. Problem Identification - The process begins when an organization recognizes that a problem which impacts its health or mission exists and change is desired. However, an organization does not always have to be in trouble to implement OD. It can also begin when the leadership has a vision to improve the organization.

2. Accepting the need for change - Once the organization has identified the need for change, it should make a decision to implement the change.

3. Assessing the Situation - Once it has been decided to implement the change, the situation needs to be assessed either by employees themselves or by consultants or experts. Some of the ways to conduct this assessment are documentation review, organizational sensing, focus groups, interviewing or surveying.

4. Planning an Intervention - Assessing, defining, and understanding the situation will lead you to the next step i.e. planning an intervention. What kind of intervention is needed depends on the nature of change required and the outcome desired. Interventions could range from training & development, team building for management or employees or establishing change teams, structural interventions or individual interventions.

5. Implementing the Intervention - After the intervention planning stage, comes its implementation.

6. Gathering data – While the intervention is being implemented and after its completion, relevant data is gathered to determine the effectiveness of the intervention. How the data would be gathered would depend on the change goals. For example, if the intervention were training and development, the data gathered would measure changes in knowledge, skills and competencies.

Through the data gathered, the organization's decision-makers determine if the intervention has met its goals. If it has, the process can end. This is depicted by the raising of the development bar. However, if the intervention has not met its goals, the decision whether to continue the cycle and carry out another intervention or to end it has to be made.

A commonly known approach of OD is the Action Research Approach which has seven phases of action as below: [3]

1. Entry of the OD practitioner - Developing the OD practitioner/leader (or client/consultant) relationship and validating the fit between them. It helps the working relationship between the practitioner and the leader(s).

2. Actual Contracting - This includes
a. clarifying the issue to be addressed (i.e., the project statement and scope)
b. determining the expectations of the leader(s) with respect to final output with timelines
c. bringing about an agreement regarding the role of the practitioner, and the leader(s) in the project
d. agreement on resources needed and accessibility of leader

3. Gathering Data & Analysis - As mentioned earlier, collecting the necessary data and analyzing it during the implementation allows the practitioner and leader(s) to understand what is happening and how to go ahead. It is also important to note that gathering the data and carrying out the diagnosis is in itself an intervention - because people will react while gathering data. Warner Burke, one of the gurus of OD, compared this to throwing a rock in the pond. One needs to be mindful of the ripples that the rock has created and not so much where the rock ends up.

Source: (3) www.cscollege.gov.sg

4. Feedback - This step involves presenting the findings and analysis along with recommendations to the leader(s). The practitioner has to make sense of the entire data so that it can be easily understood. The practitioner should also be prepared to encounter resistance while giving feedback. This is a crucial point to be tackled before any appropriate decisions can be made about how to proceed.

5.Planning Change - This step involves identifying specific courses of action (interventions) that address the situation and developing an action plan for implementation. Here, the role of the practitioner is to help facilitate the leader(s) in identifying the steps that can be taken to move the system to next steps.
Three issues should be considered while planning the intervention/s:
a. the area of the problem (culture, communication work process etc.)
b. the focus of attention (an individual, team or the complete organization)
c. mode of intervention (coaching, training and task force establishment)

6. Intervention - This refers to implementing the intervention. This is where application of change management practices would be important.

7. Evaluation - Assessing the results and determining future courses of action. Although evaluation is the last step in this approach, one needs to decide and agree what should be measured right at the beginning with the leader.

One of the characteristics of the Action Research Approach is that it helps the leader become aware of the social environment, conditions as well as the need for his/her participation. In this way, OD plays the role of a 'facilitator' rather than a 'subject matter expert'. Ensuring that the leader is aware of what is happening and his/her active involvement in the designing of the intervention is crucial.

> Successful OD efforts hinge upon high
> levels of stakeholder involvement.

The central theme of the Action Research Approach is to involve those who will be affected by the change into driving the change process.

Let's see how a multi-billion dollar global logistics company utilized OD to maintain its leadership position in the market.

Fast forward is a multi-billion dollar logistics company and an established player in the logistics market.

To counter intense competition and maintain its leadership position, it realized the need to change its organizational culture and create empowered teams which operated with autonomy, accountability and speed. The senior management accepted that this change was a necessary one and an intervention was required.

They assessed the situation and realized that this would require a sea-change from the current top-down decision-making culture of the company. The senior management would need to loosen their hold on the decision-making process currently in place. They made a plan of cultural interventions required, like opening up communication channels between functions, introducing IT systems which helped sharing of information, increasing focus on learning,

Organization Development

establishing strong teams and giving them the power to make and enforce decisions.

Next, they implemented these interventions. To support these initiatives, the organization also implemented a coaching program for leaders. A professional coach taught the top management how to appraise employee performance, help employees set goals and coach teams. As the program progressed, data was collected with the intention to let the organization's decision-makers determine whether the intervention had met its goals.

It was found that since the coaching program was integrated with the other culture change initiatives that it supported, it was a huge success. As a result of the change in the culture, stronger teams emerged and with the coaching given to the top management and better team performance, managers began to trust the teams more and empower them. In turn, the teams felt more confident in their decisions. Since the intervention had served its purpose, the process of OD ended on a successful note with the organization maintaining its competitive edge in a dynamic market.

Various roles of OD in an organization

The diagram below demonstrates why it is important for an organization to align its capabilities (along with its systems and culture) with its strategic outcomes.

(4)

Strategic goals achieved
Eg. Introduction of sound policies & delivery of quality services

⬆

Organisational capabilities developed
Eg. Robust thinking in formulating policy & timely response to customer request

↗   ↖

| Influence of organisational systems i.e. the processes & policies that provide employees with the: (1) clarity on expected behaviours; (2) ability to exhibit them; and (3) motivation to adopt them. | Influence of organisational Culture i.e. the behavioural norms in the organisation that are valued. |

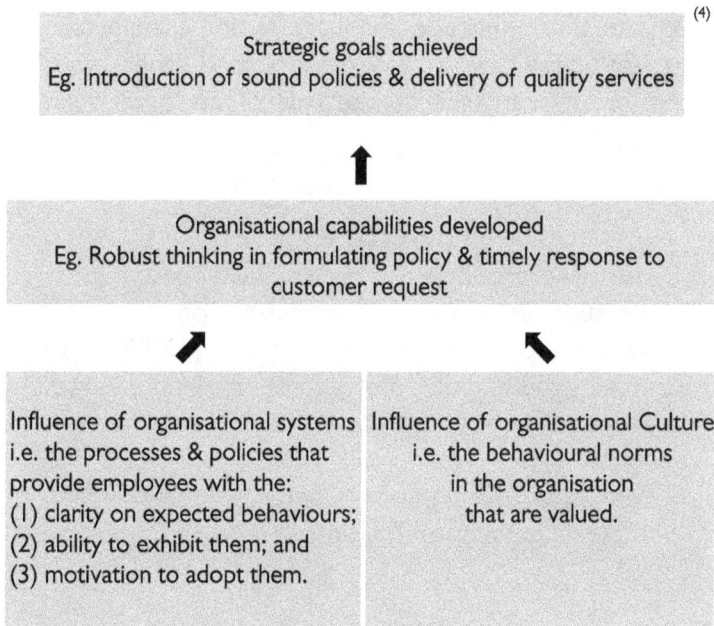

1. OD as an 'Organizational Coach' [4]

Why does an individual or a team need a coach? Just setting a goal is not enough for an individual or a team. Proper planning, preparation, guidance and training by the coach is required for them to perform to the best of their abilities, a la Shah Rukh Khan in 'Chak De India'.

OD plays a similar role by 'coaching' the organization so that it becomes capable of achieving its strategic goals. This role includes planning on a broader scale as well as implementation of internal change. In short, OD helps the organization develop and increase its internal capacities so that there is an alignment with its strategic ambition.

2. OD as an 'Organizational Counselor'

An individual often consults a counselor for a social or

Organization Development

psychological dysfunction. Similarly, during change too, an organization can face social or psychological issues. In such a scenario, OD can take up the role of an 'organizational counselor'.

Points to Ponder

1. The OD practitioner's role is a powerful one.
2. Practitioners have to alternately don caps of an 'organizational coach' - guiding the organization to its strategic goals and that of a 'counselor', pinpointing and improving the social challenges that their organization is going through.
3. Practicing OD is challenging because it means working with a complex system - the organization.

Thus, we can see that OD is a growing field that is receptive to many new approaches. HR practitioners in today's times need to develop themselves as strong change agents to help the organizational transformation process.

Caselet

OD Intervention for Team Effectiveness @ 'Shubha Bazar'

Shubha Bazar is one of the largest retail malls spread across the country. Team work was of utmost importance for their overall organizational success. Teams needed to work as part of the various departments in the retail mall.

A few years ago, it was observed by the supervisors and department managers that employee morale was low and there were lot of conflicts in the teams. All this was negatively impacting the performance of employees and the sales of each retail mall had declined sharply.

The Senior management and HR team decided to work on it by bringing in an external OD consultant. The OD consultant started work by obtaining background information from the Divisional Manager and HR managers.

The OD consultant assessed the situation with the help of HR managers by way of -
1. Survey questionnaire completed by all the staff.
2. Interview of staff members.
3. One-on one meeting with team leaders.

Post this, the OD consultant presented the findings to the Senior management and HR team. It was found that employees liked their work. Most of the team leaders and supervisors were autocratic leaders and they had low EQ. They had poor listening skills. The team based incentives distribution was not justified. There was no proper individual work allocation and accountability of work. Employees moderately trusted the store managers.

As a result of the above outcomes, the OD consultant with the help of HR managers conducted the following interventions-

1. An Employee led work group was formed to come up with suggestions and develop the recommendations for changes in the work system.
2. The OD consultant provided individual coaching to team leaders and supervisors to work on their leadership style and improve their EQ, also to communicate effectively.
3. The OD consultant conducted various team building activities and sessions for all employees to collaborate and work effectively with team members. It also covered the conflict management approaches and preferred work style.
4. The HR managers with the help of the OD consultant designed a transparent merit based incentive system for all teams and communicated it to all employees.

After working on the above interventions, a new work system and process was developed and implemented resulting into cost effective and time saving methods. There was a measurable increase in employee morale and intra and inter team co-operation. Supervisors and team leaders also started communicating effectively with their team members displaying democratic leadership styles.

The employees were aware of the transparent incentive system, so they were ready to work in teams and achieve the targets. Managers and staff members experienced less stress related to team work and observed rare conflicts. The above resulted into better performance of Shubha Bazar.

What you need to work on:
1. Why was employee morale low at Shubha Bazar a few years ago?
2. What was the role of the OD consultant in this whole process?
3. What were the outcomes for Shubha Bazar as a result of the OD interventions?
4. Are OD interventions really required in such kind of problems in an organization?

6
Change Management

> ## The only thing constant in life is CHANGE
> ## - Francois de la Rochefoucould

It's Monday morning and I'm driving to work in choc-a-bloc traffic. Suddenly, I find a diversion on the road. "Great! Just what I needed!" I mutter. When I finally get to work, I'm told that for some technical reason my desk has been shifted to the other end of the same hall.

Feeling lost, I go to my new place. It looks 'O.K.' with natural sunlight streaming in and a better view. But wait! It's not quite as cool as my earlier place. Maybe the AC here isn't powerful enough. Besides, my new neighbor is someone I have never spoken to before and the photocopy machine, printer, scanner and water cooler are all at the other end of the room. I panic, "O God! Why me? I don't want this change!"

Would you have felt the same way? Your answer would most probably be a 'yes'. The diversion in the road, we can get over. But the change in the seating arrangement is something that will disturb most of us. Why?

Generally, we respond to Change negatively or with apprehension.
And unexpected change – even more so!

Change affects people. And people do not function like machines. Pick up a machine and place it elsewhere and it will perform just fine, but that's not the case with people. People identify themselves with their organization, their departments and its processes. They create a space for themselves among their colleagues. They brand their cubicles with their own stuff. Their surroundings are a part of them. Moving them into unknown surroundings is going to unsettle

Change Management

them. It takes time for people to find their feet again. Even if this situation occurs in our personal lives, we resist the change. Then, looking at the larger picture of professional change, how do people respond to change? In most cases, the answer is, people respond to change negatively.

So don't we need change?

Of course we do. Throughout our lives we constantly experience change. The same goes for the organization, its environment, its competition, the market, the industry, and in turn for its people as well. Then the million dollar question is - How can an organization implement change yet ensure that its people adapt to the change and continue to perform successfully?

The answer lies in Change Management. It's not enough for an organization to decide to change. The change needs to be managed deftly. So what is Change Management and how does it help?

Change Management is a process through which you lead an organization through a change, for example, a merger, acquisition, rebrand, reorganization, right sizing etc. It is the approach you use to help move your organization through whatever change it is experiencing.

But before all that, we need to see what should be the perspective to handle change. We know that change is inevitable and we need to adopt it. Before accepting any change, we need to have the right approach to be a successful part of the change. Many times, this would be the situation where you are the change agent. If you have the right, rational and positive perspective, you can be an effective catalyst to lead & drive change along with others in the organization.

Why Change?

While facing challenges in professional life, the only perspective which can make you survive and grow is rationality. Whether you are in the role of a leader or a subordinate, this is the only perspective you should adopt. By clearly understanding the reasons for the change, you can direct yourself to respond (not react) to the change positively.

A rational perspective towards change can help you to embrace change in a practically stress-less manner. If you respond to change impulsively, it would be highly difficult to understand and cope with the change.

The world is changing very dynamically. Organizations have to adopt a Change Management approach not only for survival but also for growth. Obviously, continuous improvements in work methods and adapting to new technology to compete in the market are absolutely necessary.

Let's see two major reasons why many change initiatives fail -

1. But we've always done it this way!
This is what works for us!

Heard these statements before? If you haven't, you need to understand that Change in the organization affects People. People who think and feel…and not necessarily in a rational manner. Most employees dread change no matter how small it is. People are creatures of habit. They have a routine and following it gives them a feeling of familiarity and an elusive feeling of security. It becomes their comfort zone! Change is an interruption which upsets their routine and breaks their comfort zone. And very few people want to consciously break their comfort zone! Most people look at 'change' as a harbinger of uncertainty and in turn anxiety. It makes people feel disoriented.

2. Spending extra time, energy and efforts. A change throws up many challenges for employees who are already burdened with work, targets, projects and goals. It means they have even more things to accomplish with their already scarce resources - time and energy.

You must have studied the D.I.C.E factors which give us the right perspective to handle change. Let's recall and revise them.

D.I.C.E are the four factors which determine the outcome of any transformation initiative. Executives must study the four DICE factors to check if their change programs can take off or will be grounded.

I. 'D' - The duration until the change program is completed i.e. its span whether long or short and the time between assessments of milestones.

II. 'I' - The project team's performance integrity i.e. its ability to complete the change program on time. It depends on members' skills and traits relative to the project's requirements.

III. 'C' - The commitment to change displayed by the top management on the one hand and the employees affected by the change on the other.

IV. 'E' - The effort that the employees have to put in due to the change, over and above their usual work.[1]

Source: (1) [PDF]D.I.C.E (Duration, Integrity, Commitment & Effort) Framework ...
unpan1.un.org/intradoc/groups/public/documents/.../unpan022087.pdf

Worldwide changing scenario:
The dynamic forces of the global market are continuously making an impact on the business strategy of an organization. To respond to the world wide change, organizations are putting in enormous efforts. This impacts the HR strategy also. We all have to adapt to changes in this dynamic scenario. Whether you are working as senior management, middle management, or at the junior, you have to adapt the right perspective for change. It ultimately creates an impact on the overall organizational goal which is the common goal that all of us chase by performing different functions.

> "The secret of change is to focus all of your energy, not on fighting the old but on building the new." – Socrates

How to handle Change?
You must be aware of John P. Kotter's 'Eight Steps to Successful Change'. Let us revise these steps once more.

John P. Kotter is a Harvard Business School professor, leading thinker and author on organizational Change Management. Kotter's highly regarded books 'Leading Change' (1995) and the follow-up 'The Heart of Change' (2002) describe a helpful model for understanding and managing change. Each stage acknowledges a key principle identified by Kotter relating to people's response and the approach to change, in which people see, feel and then change. Kotter's eight step change model can be summarized as:

1. Increase urgency - Inspire people to move, make objectives real and relevant.

2. Build the guiding team - Get the right people in place with the right emotional commitment, and the right mix of skills and levels.

3. Get the vision right - Get the team to establish a simple vision and strategy, focus on emotional and creative aspects necessary to drive service and efficiency.

4. Communicate for buy-in - Involve as many people as possible, communicate the essentials, simply, and to appeal and respond to people's needs. De-clutter communications - make technology work for you rather than against.

5. Empower action - Remove obstacles, enable constructive feedback and lots of support from leaders - reward and recognize progress and achievements.

6. Create short-term wins - Set aims that are easy to achieve – break down tasks into smaller chunks and manageable numbers of initiatives. Finish current stages before starting new ones.

7. Don't let up - Foster and encourage determination and persistence. Encourage ongoing progress reporting and highlight achieved and future milestones.

8. Make change stick - Reinforce the value of successful change via recruitment, promotion and new change leaders. Weave change into the culture.[2]

Although there is no single methodology that can work for every company, there are some practices, tools, and techniques that can be adapted to various situations.

A Model for Change Management
Based on my experiences in the industry, I would like to put

Source: (2) www.course-iq.com

forth a model for Change Management. For any organizational development step, we need two important things. The first is the thought that we possess before designing an action plan and the second is designing the do-able action plan to execute the change. Here is the model.
Before handling the change, the leader should keep these things in mind.

1. You are working with people, which is the human capital of the organization. Please don't neglect the human approach while dealing with change. Consider all practical possibilities of responses as well as consequences of the change.

2. Clear understanding of your employees and the team is absolutely necessary to design any work plan. You should have a clear, rational SWOT analysis before beginning. The weaknesses of your team must not be a barrier for dealing with the upcoming challenges.

3. While communicating the change, each layer of the organization - the top management, the middle management and the staff should be considered equally. They must be involved, aligned to the company's vision, equipped to execute their own roles in the change process and motivated to make change happen.

4. You should possess and demonstrate complete trust in people before beginning to handle the change. You should be clearly prepared to reinforce the core messages through regular, timely communication which is rational and practical along with a human approach.

5. There should be clear thinking and identification of probable derailers.

Change Management

The do-ables based on the above thinking:
1. Start with the top management.
2. Address and involve each layer of the organization clearly.
3. Prepare a compatible action plan based on SWOT.
4. Give a rational work plan which makes people responsible and focus on result oriented tasks.
5. Address all their doubts.
6. There should be an alternative work plan for probable derailers.
7. Communicating the change message is an absolutely critical job.

Working with people ➡	Starting point should be top management Each layer of the organization should be clearly addressed.
SWOT analysis of employees ➡	Compatible action plan based on SWOT.
Involve each level of the organization ➡	Give a rational work plan which can make them responsible and focus on result oriented tasks.
Proper preparation to communicate the change ➡	Address all their doubts
Clear thinking of probable derailers ➡	There should be an alternative work plan.

Using the above steps in the suggested model, employees can understand what to expect, how to manage their own personal change in the overall change, and how to work with all others in the organization to manage and adapt to change. It is the key responsibility of the HR Manager to ensure that change is adapted positively by the employees so as to help the organization achieve its business goals.

Finally, now that we've understood Change Management, I will address an often-asked question.

Is OD the same as Change Management?
No, it isn't. There are times when an organization needs dramatic change that does not and cannot rely on the use of OD. At times, the marketplace requires that an organization take swift and unplanned actions like outsourcing, downsizing, reduction in pay or increasing health care costs. Although these changes may be absolutely necessary for its survival, they do not necessarily follow the OD processes, principles, or values.

A business needs both the OD model and the Change model for its survival. While long-term, system wide planning that results in change (the OD model) can be very beneficial for an organization and its bottom line, failure to act quickly and to take immediate decisions, even when those processes violate OD principles, may well prove to be fatal for the organization.[3]

"It is not the strongest of the species that survive, nor the most intelligent, but the one most responsive to change." - Charles Darwin

Source: (3) Organization Development by Gary McLean

Caselet

Change Management at Asia Bank

The Asia Ltd. Bank merged with Kamla Bank. Asia Bank was nearly three times the size of Kamla Bank. Asia Bank has a staff of 1200 against 2600 of Kamla Bank. More than half of the employees in Kamla Bank were clerks and around 400 were subordinate staff. There was huge gap between profiles, grades, designations and salaries of the personnel in the two banks.

With this news, the staff at Kamla Bank were insecure and felt that Asia Bank would push them to match their productivity with Asia Bank. The staff of Kamla Bank also feared that their designations and positions would be under scrutiny. There were also doubts about the continuation of rural branches of Kamla Bank as Asia Bank's business was mainly urban oriented. The apprehensions of Kamla Bank's employees were justified as both banks had altogether different cultures and management styles. While Kamla Bank concentrated on the overall profitability of the bank; on the contrary, Asia Bank converted each department to a profit center and provided bonuses for employees as per the performance of the individual profit center rather than profits of the entire bank.

Asia Bank has technologically upgraded all the Kamla Bank branches and also paid special attention to facilitate smooth integration of the two cultures. Asia Bank hired consultants to work out a uniform compensation structure and work culture to tackle the change management process.

Asia Bank had paid special attention to the behavioral

patterns of the employees to understand the level of fear and apprehension during a merger. The details are mentioned in the table below.

Post-Merger Employee Behavioral Pattern

Period	Employee Behavior
Day 1	Denial, fear, no improvement
After a month	Sadness, minor improvement
After 9 months	Acceptance, considerable improvement
After 1 ½ Years	Relief, liking, satisfaction, business development

To achieve the above acceptance and improve the employee satisfaction, Kamla Bank has considered the following important levers -
1. Database of all employees
2. Employee career maps
3. Communication tools
4. IT Integration - People Integration - Business Integration

For the above four, HR has critically managed and focused on the following:
• Employee communication
• Cultural integration
• Organization structuring
• Recruitment
• Compensation and policy rationalization
• Performance management
• Training
• Employee relations

To take care of employee resistance, the above-mentioned efforts were undertaken by Asia Bank with special emphasis on effective communication. To ensure employee participation and to decrease the resistance to change, the management of Asia Bank established clear communication channels throughout to avoid any kind of wrong messages being sent across.

Training programs (functional and soft skills) which emphasized on knowledge, technology, and attitude to upgrade skills of the employees were conducted. The management also worked on contingency plans and initiated a direct dialogue with the employee unions of Kamla Bank to maintain good employee relations. By the end of the first year of the merger, Asia Bank handled the HR challenges of Kamla Bank very well . The above HR initiatives created a win-win situation for both banks.

What you need to work on:
1. Why were Kamla Bank employees afraid after the merger?
2. Why had Asia Bank studied the employee behavioral pattern?
3. What were the steps taken by Asia Bank for smooth facilitation of the merger with Kamla Bank?
4. Is it necessary to hire a consultant for Change Management? What role did the consultants play in this case?

References-
http://www.icmrindia.org/casestudies/catalogue/Human%20Resource%20and%20Organization%20Behavior/Change%20Management-ICICI-Human%20Resource%20and%20Organization%20Behavior%20Case%20Study.htm

Change Management

7

HR Analytics

Ever felt the need to 'show them' the kind of impact HR can have on the outcomes of a business? If yes, your time's come NOW!

Enter the world of HR Analytics!

HR Analytics is a hot topic across organizations today. Also called Talent Analytics, it works to provide an organization with insights to effectively manage its people so that it can reach the business goals speedily and in an efficient manner. Basically, it means that through this process, the organization should get an optimum Return on Investment (ROI) on its people. HR Analytics applies the sophisticated techniques of data mining and business analytics for analysing the HR data.

Come to think of it, most organizations have enough data for them to effectively use HR Analytics. However, this data is not just created but also stored at various place in various different formats. Though HR Analytics softwares are quite easily available, currently many companies have a data warehouse for HR data and leverage business intelligence applications on it. Some others use data federation technology to accumulate data from different sources in one virtual database.

So What Really is HR Analytics?

The definition of Human Resource Analytics (HR Analytics) is that it is an area in the field of analytics that refers to applying analytic processes to the human resource department of an organization in the hope of improving employee performance and therefore getting a better return on investment. Let's see some characteristics of HR Analytics.[1]

Source: (1) http://www.techopedia.com/definition/28334/human-resources-analytics-hr-analytics

HR Analytics doesn't just stop at gathering data. Rather,
1. By gathering data, it delivers insights into each process of human resources and based on this relevant decisions on improving these processes can be made.
2. It correlates two kinds of data – one, people data and two – business data.
3. It establishes a direct relationship between what the HR department does and an organization's business outcomes. Strategies for improvements are then created based on this connect.
4. The core functions of HR like talent acquisition, optimization, compensation and talent development can be enriched with the application of processes in Analytics.
5. HR Analytics can be effectively used to find and address problems regarding these core functions. With its analytical workflow it acts as a guide to the management to find answers, gain insights, make decisions and take action.

Five Important HR Analytics
According to a Cornell University study, organizations today can be found collecting more of business and HR related data. However, surprisingly it is still not being used effectively to forecast workforce trends, diminish risks and add to organizational outcomes.

Rather than sticking to the past or the present, to be effective, HR Analytics must look to the future and help the organization forecast and evaluate it.

Hence, we find that of utmost importance are those HR Analytics which focus on the results produced in the human capital value chain. If you wish to know which analytics you need to use for your organization, your answer should partly be based on those which will answer the all-important question – "What impact does the HR function have on the business?"

However, there are some important areas that good analytics must focus on like:

• **Human Resources:** An organization's long-term strategies ensure that its people meet their business and career goals. Instead of viewing them as mere dimensions, these strategies can be developed further by using the analytical approaches of HR Analytics, thus creating value for the employees. So, if the organization decides to create value through employee engagement, it can identify similar people who may be engaged as a group by using a range of demographic or sociographic factors.

• **Performance:** An organization will have immense data on how many employees are in leadership positions, for what duration, the special skillsets he/she has, how many promotions to his/her credit etc. By using Analytics, the organization can identify the qualities which top performers have.

• **Leadership performance:** Through HR Analytics, an organization can analyse the factors that make its leaders effective.

• **Social capital:** In most organizations today, how the team works is more important than the skills of an individual. Taking this into account, through measures like engagement activities along with an analysis of its social network, an organization can understand which of its employees can work together in a team.

HR Analytics

• **Investment in Human Resources:** It is important for an organization to analyze how well it is investing in its human resources. As per the Cornell study, mentioned earlier, dashboards are used for the collection as well as sharing of this information. However, these should be used by HR for future planning and to predict potential problems or monitor the effect of HR practices on the workforce.

> The importance of HR analytics is now well-known across the HR fraternity. What remains is for HR leaders to gauge how to use it for their organization's benefit.

Adapting HR Analytics into today's Reality:
As I mentioned earlier, using HR Analytics to predict future performance and demonstrate the impact on businesses is the current trend in HR. However, the challenge here is that in most cases organizations are not yet sure how this can be achieved. The reason is that HR Analytics has not yet been properly defined. Another challenge is that to implement the HR Analytics approach, an organization has to get all its systems synchronised with each other. Let's look at some practical ways by which organizations can create an Analytics based HR strategy.

1. Start one step at a time -
Most organizations make the mistake of assuming that they must scrutinize their entire HR data at one time for meticulous HR analysis and a significant impact. But that's not necessary. An organization can identify and begin with a single HR process and demonstrate its impact on a crucial business outcome. A good example of this is your employee opinion survey. Here, cause-effect analytics will help you demonstrate the attitudes having a direct impact on crucial

outcomes like profitability, safety, turnover, productivity etc.

2. Begin Strong in case of Small Businesses -

A small business is devoid of 'excess baggage' like vast quantities of data and this is a distinctive advantage. Neither are they victims of old, irrelevant methods, nor do they have huge data. Due to their size, they can focus on individual performance. For them, the success of HR Analytics will depend on a strong performance-oriented culture and performance management tools.

3. Analytics for Big Organizations -

In bigger organizations, relevant data is collected at various places, servers or platforms. In this situation, Analytics needs to be conducted by gathering the data from the various different platforms behind-the-scenes.

4. Big Analytics and Huge Integration -

One can only wonder what a mammoth task integrating multiple HR platforms can be for big organizations. Here, the organization needs to put together a comprehensive approach where the analytics and its impact begin immediately on the one hand and an IT transition plan is simultaneously executed on the other. Another huge task is getting people excited about Analytics and maintaining that excitement till the data integration takes place no matter how long in terms of months or years that is. The best way to keep people motivated here is to undertake the cause-effect analytics behind the scenes and showcase the outcomes of the analytics to the leaders.

5. Strong Analytics for Integration-

One may be tempted to think that organizational costs will only go up through data warehousing. However, it is definitely useful. The challenge lies in bringing out business outcomes from other functions to display the correlation between HR and those business outcomes.

Any of these practical paths will efficiently and effectively showcase the impact of HR on actual business outcomes.

Big Data

To understand how transformation takes place through HR Analytics, let us first understand the concept of Big Data.
It is a prevalent term describing both, the availability of data (structured and unstructured) as well as exponential growth. Just as none of us can do without computers today, similar is the case with Big Data as far as its importance in the business scenario is concerned.

Why?

It's a process which comes a full circle.

More data

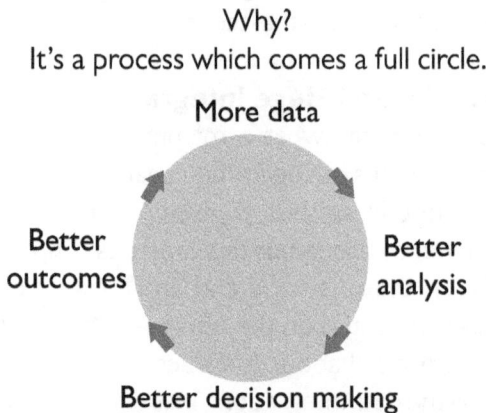

Better outcomes

Better analysis

Better decision making

According to IBM[2], "Every day, we create 2.5 quintillion bytes of data — so much so that 90% of the data in the world today has been created in the last two years alone. This data comes from everywhere: sensors used to gather climate information, posts to social media sites, digital pictures and videos, purchase transaction records, and cell phone GPS signals to name a few. This data is Big Data."

Source: (2) http://www-01.ibm.com/software/in/data/bigdata/

Some of the salient features of Big Data can be better explained as follows[3]:

1. Volume – The tremendous change in the way we live has contributed to huge volumes of data being created in various forms like unstructured data from social media, machine to machine data etc. Today, the challenge is no longer storage of huge volumes of data, rather it is -
a. Determining data relevance within these large data volumes and
b. Using Analytics for value creation from relevant data.

2. Velocity – Just as the pace of life has tremendously increased, data too comes in at break-neck speed. It presents a major challenge to organizations - to be on their toes and deal with it at the same speed through various measures like RFID tags, sensors and smart metering.

3. Variety – Since data is acquired through various areas, obviously it comes in all types of formats right from organized, numerical data from traditional databases, line-of-business applications, unstructured texts, emails, videos, audio files, stock ticker data and even financial transactions. But effectively handling i.e. handling, merging and governing different varieties of data is a major challenge for organizations.

4. Variability – An apparent issue with unstructured data is that it is variable. If the streaming in of this data is to be mapped, it would be highly inconsistent and you would have a diagram of peaks and troughs. Especially with social media, trends, events or seasons will trigger data in an absolutely unpredictable manner.

5. Complex Clean Up – Incoming data from numerous sources presents a challenge - establishing a link, finding a match, sorting for relevance and finally transforming it so that it makes sense. If these connections, correlations and multiple data linkages are not taken into consideration, you might lose your data faster than you acquire it.

Why Big Data is important?
Billions to trillions of records of millions of people across various sources like the internet, sales, customer service, social media, cell phone data and so on is collected. This is typically unstructured data that is often incomplete.

Truly speaking acquisition of large amounts of data is not the problem. The real question is what you want to achieve with all that data. Most organizations would answer this question by saying that they would like to use this data for improving business outcomes be it by reducing costs and time, better decision making, or new product development and smarter offerings. But that's not all. An organization can undertake all the following by combining Big Data with Analytics:
• **Cost Saving -** Diving deep to determine causes of failure, cropping up of issues and defects in near-real time, thus saving costs.

• **Logistics -** Improve logistics by optimizing routes for package delivery vehicles even while they are on the move.

• **Maximizing Profits -** Analyzing SKUs (Stock Keeping Unit) to determine prices that maximize profit and reduce inventory carried.

• **Retail -** Generating retail coupons at the point of sale (POS) based on the customer's current and previous purchases.

• **Sales** – Creating tailor-made recommendations for mobile devices when customers enter a specific area so that they can take advantage of attractive offers.

• **Risk Management** - Recalculate entire risk portfolios in minutes.

• **Customer Management** - Swiftly detect customers who are the most serious and important.

• **Control** - Using Clickstream Analysis and Data Mining to detect fraudulent behavior.[3]

> If you thought Big Data today is terabytes, think again! Though it would probably change as we progress further, today Big Data is Petabytes which is 1,024 Terabytes or to go further, Exabytes which is 1,024 Petabytes.

Transformation through Big Data and HR Analytics – A boon to organizations

With the acquisition and analysis of Big Data, organizations have benefitted by an increase in revenues, improved understanding of and accurately targeting customers and cutting costs through better business processes.

Big Data also helped HR managers analyze tons of structured and unstructured data to address employee productivity, impact of training, predictors of workforce attrition, and identification of leadership potential.

Source: (3) http://www.sas.com/en_us/insights/big-data/what-is-big-data.html

HR Analytics

But this is not to say that HR Analytics is being used well across organizations for various HR functions. As per a survey by a talent analytics software vendor SHL in 2013, more than 77% of HR professionals are still unable to determine how their organization's workforce potential is affecting the bottom line, while less than half i.e. 44% use objective data regarding talent performance to guide business decisions. Thus, many fail to use data analytics for identification and development of star performers.

If this is the problem, how can organizations use HR Analytics for personnel decisions?
For this, acquiring the relevant software is the first step. It is followed by determining your goal and choosing an HR Analytics vendor accordingly. For example, if your requirements are quite specific, a smaller vendor would more likely give you customized solutions at reasonable costs.

Finding Analysis Super-jocks
Again just installing HR Analytics software is of no use if members of the HR team cannot mine and interpret data. Who would have thought that the HR department would require data management experts and analysis super-jocks. Of course, you may need to partner with the IT guys, but often, not having an expert in the department can turn into a serious disadvantage.

To overcome this problem, some innovative organizations have hired data scientists to work and even lead HR departments. A case in point is General Motors which has recently hired a visiting scientist at MIT Media Lab with a Ph. D in engineering and a Six Sigma Black Belt as its Head of Global Talent and Organizational Capability.

**How organizations can benefit
from HR Analytics software**

Reducing recruitment cost per hire

Analysing failure reasons of new hires

Reducing employee turnaround rate

Analysing e-learning abandonment rate

Reducing bonus compensation rate

To conclude, with HR Analytics, leaders and managers have immense opportunities to use talent data in showcasing the difference that HR makes to the outcomes of a business.

■■■

HR Analytics

Caselet

HR Analytics @ Rohit International Limited

Rohit International Limited is in the business of marketing and sales of Diamonds and Gold. The company has grown since the last 25 years and recently acquired Geeta International which is into similar business. The HR team faced many challenges to integrate the employees of both the companies. It was a tough challenge to manage the talent of the organization during this period.

For any company, it's very important to manage talent effectively and develop the existing talent pool for success. The company required specific marketing skills and product knowledge for which management trainees had to go through an intensive training for one year. Employees had to obtain certification in examining the real diamonds. Since the company trained their employees in a unique way, the employees were retained in the company for a longer period of time.

The company had low attrition over the years. Most employees would superannuate in the same time frame. As a result, the company will face shortage of talent soon. With this foresighted challenge, the HR team requested the Management to tie up with an IT Company who would provide Workforce Analytics Software and Services.

The company deployed an integrated HR Management Software which included Performance and Goal Management, Compensation, Recruiting Management, and Career Development and Planning. This software was able to provide powerful workforce analytics and planning solutions with reporting abilities to help strategic planning.

The Workforce Analytics Module has enabled the HR team of Rohit International Limited to model several turnover scenarios to quantify the impact of the retirement surge. The HR team is armed with the knowledge of 'What-if' scenarios. The HR team could plan proactively to address this issue. The HR Analytics module enabled the HR team to quantify and document the need for talent management strategies. Even other modules like career planning, compensation management and performance management helped the HR team to manage the performance cycle seamlessly.

Annual performance reviews of all employees were completed in a timely manner. Merit pay was processed using information directly from performance reviews, enabling a pay for performance system.

With this new process, the company had the ability to track the progress and could reach 100% compliance on annual reviews. It also helped the company manage talent effectively and drive performance along with effective recruitment using workforce analytics.

What you need to work on:
1. Why did the company implement a new Workforce Analytics module?
2. What was the HR challenge that Rohit International was facing?
3. "Workforce analytics has made the HR manager's life easy." Comment.

References-
http://www.successfactors.com/content/dam/successfactors/en_us/resourc
es/case-studies/black-hills-cs.pdf

HR Analytics

8

Exit (Bye Bye)

All the Best!

Take care!.............................Keep in touch!

Famous last words from ex-colleagues!

Anyone who has worked in the corporate sector would know that these words signify the beginning of the end of an employee's tenure in an organization.

Goodbye's are always difficult whether it is a neighbor, a dear one or an employee. With employees though, the situation is not just "difficult", it is also "delicate". So much so, that most organizations have a proper 'goodbye' or exit process.

Yes, I'm talking about Employee Exit Management. Generally, it applies to those who have resigned as well as to those who have been terminated by the company, or in case of redundancy too. In case of a termination or redundancy, the organization has to be extra careful not to leave any loose ends while concluding its association with the employee.

Types of Employee Exits
Employee exits can be classified into four types based on whether they are good or bad for both, the company and the employee.

1. The Lose-Lose Exit: This exit brings about a break in a mutually beneficial relationship. The exit is unfortunate for both, the company and the employee. For e.g. an employee may leave because of relocation to another city where the company doesn't have its offices; or an employee may have to leave due to a disability or illness.

2. The Lose-Win Exit: The company loses but the

employee gains. This happens when a good employee who is valuable for the company leaves for greener pastures (a better role/more money/future growth opportunities/better work culture.)

3. The Win-Lose Exit: Now the company gains but the employee loses. For e.g. an employee is fired for reasons of unethical or immoral conduct or non-performance.
Now the best one at last...

4. The Win-Win Exit: This is a good exit for both, the company and the employee. For e.g. a misfit or an underperformer realizes his/her lacunae and the need to better his/her skills and leaves for further education.[1]

There is a standard model of a four-phase process of Employee Exit Management. It consists of:
1. Knowledge Transfer Questions (creating the background for employee transition)
2. Operational Responsibilities (basic housekeeping)
3. Standardized Exit Survey (documenting employee impressions)
4. Face-to-Face Exit Interview (personal and professional closure)

1. Knowledge Transfer Questions
One of the best ways of acquiring crucial 'how to' knowledge from an exiting employee is by using knowledge transfer questions. I highly recommend that the knowledge transfer process is initiated well before the time the employee actually leaves. This knowledge can help the replacement and improvement of the organization's Standard Operating Procedures (SOPs). The following steps can ensure a clean knowledge transfer.

Source: (1) http://www.qualtrics.com/research-suite/employee-exit-interviews/

1. For information which is not of a confidential nature, ask the exiting employee to sort the information into appropriate files (both hard and soft copies) into shared folders or a document library.

2. Ask them to trim this information, classify these files and make notes for their successors. The notes would include information on roles and task folders.

3. Go back to his/her job description or even the annual performance plan and appraise the important tasks which the person performs. These notes can help you in your discussions with the employee on how he/she goes about his/her tasks, the knowledge and skills needed for the job and the risks and pitfalls to be aware of.

4. Make it a point to discover their network of contacts and sources of knowledge.

5. The best way is to make way for a 'live' handover between the outgoing employee and his/her successor.

Though this tool has often gone unnoticed, using it has many advantages. Firstly, it ensures that knowledge crucial to the organization is not lost by an employee's exit. Secondly, absolutely useful for new employees, it helps shorten their learning curve.

2. Operational Responsibilities
Once the knowledge transfer is done, it's down to brass tacks – the practical issues of departure. Either a day before or on the day of departure, the outgoing employee cleans up his space, desk, computer and hands over the company returnables like I-card, company badge, laptop etc. These form part of the exit formalities.

3. Standardized Exit Survey
An outgoing employee's general impressions and

Exit (Bye Bye)

perceptions and his/her reasons for leaving are a goldmine of information and insights for the organization. Of course for it to be of use, this information has to be collected in a standardized format. No less important than other lawful assessments, Employee Exit Surveys have to be at par with professional testing standards and legal requirements.

The basic idea is to use the insights from this information for improvement on various issues like SOPs, incentive programs, organizational structure, managerial approach etc.

4. Face-to-Face Exit Interview

Why should an organization spend its time listening to employees who shall no longer be working with them?
Answer: They should if they want to know what they don't know about themselves.

The four phase process of Employee Exit Management ends with the employer and employee concluding the association with a face-to-face exit interview.

What are the Measures to be used for an Employee Exit Interview?

Employee exit interviews must be used as a tool to detect possible problems in employee engagement and retention. They are a useful tool to indicate the exact reasons that employees want to leave. What are the underlying issues? Is it unfulfilled expectations, problems in work profiles or organizational culture? The answers that you are trying to get must give you insights on how to retain your employees. Considering this, the following points can be used as

measures or indicators for an Employee Exit Interview:
• Job Description, job responsibilities and actual performance
• Mentoring programs undertaken
• Work environment and conditions, organization and work culture
• Prospects for progress, acquiring and improving skills and career growth
• Training programs
• Job satisfaction
• Team Dynamics
• Distribution of Work
• Flexibility the job offers in terms of schedules and location of work
• Compensation and Benefits

How to conduct exit interviews?
In my opinion, there is only one way – the hard way – face-to-face. Only face-to-face interviews offer the opportunity to truly communicate, comprehend and interpret, probe and get to the root of sensitive or reluctant feelings. To prepare for a face-to-face exit interview, it is best to be planned. Have a proper questionnaire ready and enough space for notes where needed. Be clear as to who will use the knowledge and how, before you begin to collect it. Knowledge must not be collected for knowledge's sake; it has to be useful. Organize a time and place suitable to both – the interviewer and interviewee which shall help to avoid interruptions.
Apart from this, you must be clear about-

What?
What are the areas of information that you would like to have information about?

Exit (Bye Bye)

Who?

Who will you choose as the interviewer? Traditionally this role was performed by someone from HR. But if you are going to choose someone else, consider his/her interview and interpersonal techniques and also how open, neutral and honest he/she is. If you want the employee's boss or a senior colleague to do the job, consider the employee's relationship with them. No matter who you select, they must be trained and skilled to carry out the job.

Why?

Exit interviews help obtain useful knowledge that the organization would have otherwise lost like contacts, links, insights, tips and experience. These may or may not be useful to the outgoing employee but are life blood to his/her successors and the organization. Most people who are leaving would be open for a knowledge transfer, whether as a meeting between the employee and the replacement or even during the exit interview.

How?

a. While conducting the interview, go into the role of the listener. Remember it's the employee's turn to talk.
b. Let the employee take his/her time to open up.
c. Persuade him/her to express themselves where necessary but do not pressurize. If you do, they might simply clam up.
d. Reassuring them that the information will not be used to harm them will also go a long way
e. Be neutral. Don't argue or agree. Remember you are here to obtain views, valuable feedback and answers
f. Understand what the person is trying to express
g. Be aware of non-verbal signals like body-language, facial expressions etc.
h. Respond but do not react

The 3 E's

In some organizations, exit interviews are a part of a series of "cradle-to-grave" interviews. They aim at collecting knowledge using the 3E's i.e. Entry, Expert and Exit. As their names suggest, 'Entry Interviews' collect knowledge right after an employee joins. The organization benefits from the employee's new and fresh perspective. The new joinee is also asked what help he/she needs to 'speed up'. The organization conducts 'Expert interviews' when these employees have acquired and developed the required skills and are experts in their fields.

Points to Ponder

- Exit interviews are generally used for people who want to resign voluntarily or those who are retiring. A very different approach would have to be used for someone who has been asked to leave or has been laid-off. However, I feel everyone who leaves must be given the opportunity of an exit interview.
- An exit interview also provides the employee the chance to 'reconsider'. If this really happens, and the organization would like to retain them, make sure you act swiftly and take advantage of this opportunity.
- Study the answers of the interview. Analyse and interpret them in a rational and detached way.
- Prepare to take action as required. Report your feedback on the exit interview to the relevant leader/leadership team & HR. If there is an urgent issue or some checking or follow-up is required, ensure you do it and report that too accordingly.

Exit (Bye Bye)

Exit Interviews - Aims and Outcomes
Why would an organization like to hear bitter home-truths from someone they won't be working with anymore?
Because, it's like strong medicine!

The very reason that exit interviews are conducted is that the organization needs to know why its talent on whom it has spent huge amounts of time, energy and money for acquisition, development and management wants to leave, taking their skills and competencies elsewhere.

1. Make Peace, Not War - Exit interviews help an organization 'make peace' with displeased employees and ensure that they do not leave with a revengeful attitude. No doubt this creates a positive impact on the employee leaving the organization who feels heard. It lets him/her voice his/her opinions and it's a big relief to people to 'get it off their chest'. The exit interview is the employee's chance to have their say regarding:
a. The reason they want to leave
b. Their opinions about the work environment and the organization
c. Areas of improvement
d. Satisfaction levels
e. Their contribution to the organization

2. Positive Work Culture - Exit interviews signal that the organization is ready to listen. It is the sign of a positive work culture. When you ask someone why he/she wants to leave, you are stating that while you respect his/her decision, you are eager to understand what went wrong. It shows your organization's openness to introspection.

3. Enhances Manager's Understanding – The

organization gets information from the 'horse's mouth'. People managers can learn a lot about managing people from the valuable feedback that exit interviews generate. Learning from feedback is a powerful process of growth & development.

4. Retaining a valuable employee – If a valuable employee's resignation has been accepted easily or if earlier discussion/s hasn't/haven't been fruitful, the exit interview is the last chance to prevent such an employee from leaving by clearing the air. *Aisa mauka baar baar nahin aayega!*

5. Support to HR practices - Exit interviews are among the essential HR practices for an organization. Most organizations use data from exit interviews for planning training and development processes. They also provide guidelines on improving recruitment and induction of new employees. Most important is their contribution to improving employee retention. It also indicates the need for Succession Planning. Valuable talent often leaves in search of opportunities for learning, growth and development, at times in spite of being paid well in their organizations. If this is happening in your organization, it's something you will have to work on very fast.

While some in the organization are waiting for an opportunity, others at higher levels may be overburdened with responsibilities. Both these situations are excellent reasons for your talent to leave. An exit interview will help you identify if this is what is happening. Accordingly, you can take steps to work on growth and development and handing over additional responsibilities to deserving employees on the one hand and work on delegation on the other hand to ensure equitable distribution of work and opportunities.

Exit (Bye Bye)

6. Avoiding Unfortunate Loss of Talent – Exit interviews may throw up a variety of reasons that may take the organization completely by surprise. Job dissatisfaction, lack of appreciation, poor management practices, lack of growth opportunities and yes, harassment and conflict too. Exit interviews are a wake-up call for employers to realize what's wrong and act on it so that it doesn't affect talent which they have painstakingly nurtured.

Conclusion

An Employee Exit Process must aim at final closure and concluding the association between the employee and the organization without any loose ends, and on a positive professional note. Employee Exit Management provides immense learning opportunities for organizations to evaluate, question and improve their SOPs. It is important to invest time in the designing and implementation of an effective exit process to ensure a healthy contribution to the company's business outcomes and culture.

Dealing with the results of Employee Exit Interviews

All right! Now we know that the importance of Exit Interviews cannot be overemphasized. But the next question is how does one deal with the results of the exit interviews?

Smart organizations will make use of these results in the following ways:
• To make improvements in employee retention strategies to ensure reduced employee turnover.
• Create a yardstick to check where they stand within the industry for each item on the exit interview.
• To compare and check for co-relation between exit interviews and employee engagement surveys, both quantitatively and qualitatively.

• To track movement in employee satisfaction levels by analysis of exit interview data. This is an indicator of improvements made in the company.

Increasing Responses for Exit Interviews

A survey states that only about a third of the employees exiting, complete an exit interview. Of course your exiting employee has nothing to lose. It's in your interest to ensure that each employee completes the exit interview.

The organization's HR policy must accordingly make exit interviews a priority for managers. Here are other methods which can help you:

1. If face-to-face interviews don't work for your organization, try to go online. People may be more frank in an online interview.

2. If you are talking to someone who has been asked to go, be aware of the questions you are asking and your responses. You might touch a live wire.

3. Reassure respondents that their comments and honest feedback will not be openly shared and they need not fear damaged relationships with their ex-bosses or colleagues or any harm with future employer/s.

4. If the organization has a culture of responding on exit interviews, you may want to thank these employees for an honest appraisal. You may try to highlight the difference their opinions have made in terms of changes implemented in the organization.

5. Get a third party to audit the Exit interview process independently.

> If you want to know how your organization fares on its Employer Value Proposition, the best place to search is an Exit Interview!

Caselet

Hitesh's Case of Exit and Come Back

Hitesh was the best student of a premier business school. He secured final placement through the college placement cell in a leading sales & marketing company in Pune. He joined the company, settled in well, came up with innovative ideas which were recognized and implemented.

He was the best employee in the organization from day one. His performance was excellent and he was well accepted by his colleagues and seniors. He was achieving the targets very well and also helping his colleagues. Mr. Ravat was his immediate boss and he was very happy with Hitesh's performance. Mr. Ravat gave him an excellent hike in his salary after completion of his probation period of one year. Hitesh enjoyed working in Mr. Ravat's department. He liked the open culture and freedom provided by the company. He felt lucky to work with a company having such a wonderful culture.

But he started facing a problem when Mr. Ravat was promoted and transferred to Mumbai office and the new boss Mr. Vivek Kumar took charge. Mr. Kumar did not give any freedom to the staff. He had a control and command style of managing the team. He micro-managed which was not liked by anybody at the Pune office. He monitored employees on an hourly basis and even shouted at them every now and then. He wanted employees to report to him several times in a day which was different from keeping him informed.

With such an environment, everyone in the Pune branch was demoralized and not performing well. Mr. Kumar targeted

Hitesh as he tried to give some suggestions in a meeting. He shouted at him in the presence of all employees in the meeting. On the same day, Hitesh resigned from the company. Many employees like Hitesh left the Pune branch.

After two years of working with another organization, Hitesh once again wants to join the Pune branch of his earlier company in a larger role and at a more senior position, as he has got to know that Mr. Ravat is back again as Branch Head in Pune.

What you need to work on:
1. Is there a need of exit interviews in the above mentioned situation?
2. Why does Hitesh want to come back to the same company?
3. What is the role of HR in the above-mentioned situation?
4. If you were Hitesh, what would you do?

Exit (Bye Bye)

9

Strategic Human Resource Management

What should be the outcome of all things HR?
To support business goals and objectives through effective Talent Management.

All processes, policies and procedures that an organization follows are important due to the effect they have on 'people' who are instrumental in helping an organization achieve its goals and objectives. Time and again, I have emphasized in this book that 'people' matter.

My first job was that of a management trainee in the Industrial Relations function on the shop floor of a petrochemical company. My mentor, Mr. Sujit Mane was the Plant Technical Head. The first thing he told me to do after introducing the plant, the technical manufacturing process and key people was to observe the workers and strike a bond with them and wonder of wonders...that too while they were in the canteen! He told me to specially observe them after they had their first morsel of food.

If you are amazed, I was doubly so! You see, the secret is that the quality of food is the cause of many worker-related problems. I was lucky to have learnt my first HR lesson – 'A Content worker/employee is an Asset', at a very young age. To this day, it remains the most important lesson I have learnt in my life! My observations helped me gain an insight into the workers' minds.

Though I was not involved in creating the Strategic HRM model for the company, at the time, I learnt to look at it with the right perspective. Today, after 18+ years of experience, I have realized that everything to do with Talent (Acquiring, Developing, Managing, Retaining) is the core part of Strategic HRM.

Strategic HR Management

Strategic Human Resource Management shows the clear path for the development of the *modus operandi* of all HR processes. It is aligned and linked to the business strategy because both are informative and their outcomes are totally interdependent.

A good business strategy takes in continuous inputs about human capital. The business strategy is shaped, based on the skills and knowledge which is available to the organization and the way in which this talent needs to be managed. Nowadays business strategies, are inseparable from and are linked to Strategic HRM and so are individual HR strategies. For instance, if the business strategy is to better the customer experience, the individual HR strategy may be to enhance relevant training for the executives.

So simply put, Strategic Human Resource Management is an approach to HR management that provides a strategic framework for the organization to achieve its long-term business goals.

What is Strategy?
The word 'Strategy' is derived from the concepts of Military. Strategy is the core part of any management which determines the direction in which the organization is going in relation to its environment and helps you work out a clear action plan based on observation and analysis. In our schooldays, we all studied History but most of us didn't understand why we had to study something that was over and done with. I feel, the importance of History is that it teaches us the approach to analyze past track records. Further, we use it in future strategy planning and designing.

Strategy planning and designing is totally dependent upon three things:
1. Who are we - Knowing and Defining (SWOT-Internal and External)
2. Where do we want to go - QUO VADIS, and after answering these two questions, we derive the approach -
3. How can we get there? (Action plan laying out methods to be adopted, processes and tools to be deployed etc.)

This goes for any strategic model in the world. Strategy may not always be written down formally, but may come about by actions and reactions. It defines the organisation's behavior and how it plans to deal with its environment. Its about the future state and helps steer the organization ahead.

What is Strategic HRM?
Coming back to our topic, Strategic HRM is based on three things.
1. Business Goals of the organisation
2. Understanding the product, market, brand, its SWOT analysis and
3. The clear aligned reflection of these in the overall HR strategy.

As I mentioned, Talent and People Management is the core part of HR. People Management begins with talent acquisition, its development, management and retention. Every company needs best employees who give optimum performance which contributes to the overall business goals. Organizations spend huge amounts on appropriate compensation, rewards and trainings. Every company has different value systems, work structures, cultures, quality standards, and different target markets for their products.

Strategic HR Management

So the areas involved in Strategic HRM are Hiring, Talent Compensation, working with employees in a collaborative manner to boost Retention, Improving the quality of work experience, Maximizing the mutual benefit of employment for the employer and employee.

Considering this wide scope, the strategic role of HR becomes extremely crucial since it ultimately reflects on business goals.

What should be the end result of Strategic HRM?
To support business goals and objectives through effective Talent Management.

The Role of Strategic Human Resource Management in Business
HR as a function is becoming more and more dynamic and is getting refined by the day. It is becoming more and more strategic in nature and key to achieving organizational goals.

Earlier, HR was limited to being just a manpower planning function. It acted as an input to the company's annual budget and was largely a data-driven effort to managing number of employees and their cost. No longer are businesses so simple. With their increasing complexity and diversity of business spread over multiple locations, Strategic Talent Planning (STP) has become a focus area for Strategic HRM.
STP is a process by which HR determines
a) The type of talent required for a particular job at a given location and
b) The cost of such talent

It helps to make sure that the organization is equipped with the **Right Talent at the Right Time for the Right Job.**

Strategic Talent Planning helps organizations maintain flexibility and manage change required. It also helps the organization deal with socio-economic, technological and legislative trends in the industry that the organization functions in.

Points to Ponder for Strategic Talent Planning

• Where is the organization headed?

• What are the skills that our talent must have?

• How can we develop HR Strategies to fill in this gap?

HR compares the existing talent vis-à-vis the required talent portfolio. The gap in the talent can either be sourced from within if available or from outside the company. Thus, STP helps a company to understand and forecast the type and the cost of talent required.

STP requires HR to collate and integrate details of existing and required talent across the organization and that's not easy. Try doing it for an organization with just 500 employees! For HR to add value to the talent planning process, its members need to know business goals, operating plans/budgets, possess broad analytical and finance skills and have a macro view of the business.

The moot point is how many HR professionals possess these skills? The answer is very few!

Why? As per my experience, neither their education nor on-

Strategic HR Management

the-job training are able to provide them with the complete knowledge of key business drivers and analysing numbers.

Challenges in Strategic HRM

In the scenario that we live in, the world market is changing at break-neck speed. Customers are getting better choices for their needs. Naturally customer loyalty towards brands has started declining. Everybody is under pressure, be it employers, employees, markets, brands. The outcome of this pandemonium is the World "War for Talent" (which has cropped up even before the World "War for Water"). This again has happened due to:

1. Plethora of options available with talent today
2. Employees need to cope with tremendous work pressure
3. Head-hunters are finding it difficult to recruit global talent
4. The interest-span of employees has reduced
5. Employee loyalty is slowly becoming extinct
6. Presence of several interest groups and stakeholders who need to be managed deftly

Thus, HR departments of companies are constantly facing the challenge of aligning HRM activities and policies to business strategies.

Some Strategic HRM Models -

Most of us are familiar with the theory of Strategic HRM, describing different approaches/models of its development and implementation. Let's see them here again.

1. The High Performance Management Model:

A well-known definition of the high-performance work system was produced by the US Department of Labor (1993). The High Performance Management Model focuses on the progress of various related areas which, put together have an impact on an organization's outcomes. These could be areas like productivity, growth, profits, customer service etc. which finally result in an increase in value to stakeholders. It would also include rigorous recruitment and selection procedures, incentive pay systems and performance management processes. High performance management practices include:

1. Developing employee skills and imparting training and management development programs with a view to self-management and increasing team capabilities. This will help improve organizational performance.

2. Aligning the processes – strategic, operational and those of people management with organizational objectives. This will help foster trust, engagement and commitment to the overall organizational goals.

3. Decentralizing the decision making process so as to ensure faster decisions by those who are in touch with the customer.

4. Engaging with the community outside the organization. This fosters both commitment and trust within and outside the organization.

Of course, high performance requires vision, sound leadership, bettering employee skills and employee engagement. Leadership will give a sense of momentum and direction.

II. The High Commitment Management Model:

High-commitment management has been described by Wood (1996) as: 'A form of management which is aimed at eliciting a commitment so that behavior is primarily self-regulated rather than controlled by sanctions and pressures external to the individual, and relations within the organization are based on high levels of trust.'

As the name suggests, the High Commitment Management Model aims at getting a commitment from people so that their behavior and actions are self-regulated instead of being bound or restricted by the organization's hierarchy or policies.

In this model, the levels of employee commitments are high and relationships are based on trust. Let's see the approaches that create a high commitment organization:

1. Achieving flexibility and doing away with rigidity; reducing hierarchies.

2. Emphasis on growth and development, commitment and training and development of employees.

3. High emphasis of employees on quality management.

4. Heavy reliance on teamwork and problem solving in teams (quality circles).

5. Better assessment and compensation structures with emphasis on profit sharing and merit-based pay.

6. Enhancing job descriptions/ Enlarging/ Enriching roles to improve job satisfaction of employees.

7. Cushioning employees against uncertainties like lay-offs or redundancies. Working on permanent employee guarantees and using temporary workers to manage fluctuating demand for labour.

III. High Involvement Management Model:

This approach focuses on ensuring that employees are highly involved and engaged. It fosters clear lines of communication to ensure clear and continuous dialogue between the managers and their team members to achieve clarity on expected performance. So, people are treated as partners instead of employees and are encouraged to speak up about what matters.

With high involvement, everyone has a clear understanding

of what is to be achieved. Also, this gives a framework to ensure that goals will be achieved. The practices which are identified with the High Involvement Management Model are 'Online' work teams, 'Offline' employee involvement activities, problem solving through group interaction, Job rotation, Suggestion schemes and Decentralization of quality efforts.

Thus in summary, by impacting the various facets of HR like recruitment, training and development, compensation, succession planning etc., Strategic HRM helps an organization develop an edge over competition in terms of talent readiness and capability in the long run.

■ ■ ■

Strategic HR Management

Caselet

Give HR its Due – Strategic Importance

Eshan, the new Human Resources Head at Vishal Manufacturers was not happy with the way the company was managing its employees and the way the Human Resources (HR) Department was viewed by the management. He felt that in the era of globalization, an organization should change its style of functioning. The HR Department was involved only in day to day administrative activities. The management never involved the HR Head in the business strategy meetings.

Eshan was aware that in most of the good companies including his previous organization, HR was considered as a key department to develop and retain talent. He observed that Vishal Manufacturers was far behind in involving the HR Department in key strategic plans and decisions. He wanted to interact with & impress upon the management about the important role that the HR department must play in setting future direction for the organization, improving employee performance, defining skill sets needed etc.

Finally, soon he got the opportunity to meet the senior management as he had been called to the Head Office to discuss the cost and administrative aspects of recruiting staff in the maintenance department. Eshan decided to grab the opportunity and make the maximum use of this meeting. He requested the senior team for permission to present an important issue which would benefit the company in the long run. In the presentation, he highlighted the high turnover in the maintenance department and other important departments at Vishal Manufacturers. He was upfront and conveyed that Senior Managers deployed command and control style of management. This was an old style and he requested this senior team to provide autonomy and freedom to the managers of all departments which would make the managers' work interesting and challenging. He mentioned that standardization, uniformity and compliance would not work in the current era. Senior managers needed to be more flexible and involve members of the department in planning & delivery of enhanced output. He also conveyed the key role of Human Resources in strategic decisions of business. He requested the management to look into his viewpoints and consider them favourably. After his presentation, he discussed the main agenda for which he was called with respect to the hiring in the maintenance department and thanked them for listening to his views and experience candidly.

Though the management thinking was conventional since they were all old timers in the organisation, they were open enough to consider Eshan's views. After a week's time, he received a call from a senior team member to attend the executive committee meeting and provide a detailed presentation on the strategic role of Human Resources and the steps to integrate the HR function in the strategic planning process of the organisation.

What you need to work on:
1. Why was the HR Department not given strategic importance at Vishal Manufacturers?
2. What did Eshan share with the Senior Team ?
3. What challenges will Eshan face to establish the strategic importance of the Human Resources function?
4. Why should HR be involved in the business strategy formulation at Vishal Manufacturers?

Strategic HR Management

10
Challenges in Today's Human Resource Management

We have already seen that as per Adam Smith, 'the market moves through invisible hands.'

Today however, you will find that there is no longer just one market. With companies setting up their presence all over the world, there are various markets globally and all of them have just one thing in common - they change at break-neck speed.

If one studies right from the time of the Industrial Revolution, till today, the change in scenario can be summed up as follows:

The Organization	Old Scenario	Today
1.Focus	Production	Customer
2.Aim	Profit Making	Customer Delight
3.Means	Standardization /Cost Cutting	Employee Delight

If you were surprised on reading Employee Delight, don't be! The path of achieving the goal of a delighted customer begins with having a happy employee. While the Marketing function is focused on the customer, the HR function is focused on employees. If you look closely, you will find similarities between the two functions - Marketing and HR :

1. While there is stiff competition for acquiring customers, there is equally stiff competition for acquiring(hiring) employees.

2. Both are smart and have plenty of choice.

3. Both are equally demanding.

4. Both, customer loyalty and employee loyalty are diminishing.

Challenges in Today's HR Management

> An employee is the internal customer
> for the HR function.

Dynamic and growing global markets, demanding customers, constant changes in technology and the way business is done, and hugely talented but equally choosy employees - organizations have their work cut out for them. So while organizations face these challenges, how is HR placed today?

In earlier times, along with the other departments, HR too was a static function. Needless to say, today, it is not just dynamic, it is also business driven.

> People across various backgrounds –
> educational, financial, socio-cultural are
> thrown together constantly to work
> towards a common goal and this is the
> biggest challenge that HR faces.

So what are the various challenges that HR as a function faces today? In my view, these challenges can be classified under two heads -
1. Strategic goals (Macro View)
2. Actionables (Micro View)

I. Strategic Goals (Macro View) – These challenges are at the macro level – strategic level of the organization.

a. Return on Investment – The best way to assess a function's performance is to find out its contribution to the business. HR today has to ensure the best Return on the organization's investment in its people.

b. Success and Value Addition – Each function has to

perform and HR is no different. The success of the HR department can be measured by outcomes which determine the success of the organization like conflict resolution, placing the right person in the right job at the required time, and also the value addition that HR makes to the organization in making it a better place to work.

c. Compensation and Benefits – HR faces the challenge of assuring each employee of fair compensation and benefits. The HR strategy regarding employee compensation and benefits will determine its success at Talent Acquisition and Retention.

d. Company Strategy, Goals, and Culture – The overall HR strategy and each element thereof must be aligned to and supportive of the organizational strategy. HR has to ensure that the strategies, goals and culture of the organization percolate down to each and every employee and are upheld by the HR leaders themselves.

e. Diversity and Equality – Managing a diverse, global workforce is one of the key challenges of HR today. While diversity needs to be encouraged as an organizational strategy ; while hiring, it is important for HR to keep in mind that potential hires need to fit in with their respective customers and colleagues. At the same time, HR should make sure that equality is maintained and no employee is treated unjustly based on socio-cultural or gender based factors.

f. Mergers and Acquisitions, Technological changes, Rightsizing – An organization may change its ownership, technology or its way of functioning in response to market forces, without giving employees the time or space to adapt or adjust. At such times, it is the HR's responsibility to help employees deal with and overcome the anxiety such situations create. In such a scenario, HR's role is to make sure that teams are equipped both, mentally and knowledge wise to deal with the change. At such times, HR may need to focus on training and development to equip employees with the new required skillsets.It will also need to don many hats like those of career counsellor, change agent, partner etc. HR will also need to change its policies so as to align them to the needs of the changing organization.

Above, we saw the challenges that HR will face today strategy-wise. Now, let us look at the challenges that it will face in the form of actionables (day-to-day functioning) on the ground.

2. Actionables (Micro View) –

a. Talent Acquisition, Talent Retention, Talent Management – These are never-ending challenges. There is a continuous need for HR to plan the organization's need for talent. For this, it must take stock of the capabilities of its talent. Or else, it may find that what it has achieved by hiring people, could have been easily achieved by training the existing staff. Even while trying to retain an employee, HR should be sure that the organization will indeed benefit by retaining the employee. Talent Acquisition, Retention and Management must be in tandem with the business strategy.

b. Attrition – Curbing attrition rates is a nightmare for the HR function no matter which industry. Not only does HR have to ensure that it has its basics like Compensation & Benefits right, it also has to find ways to get employees to effectively engage with the organization. Many organizations have tailor-made employee engagement programs for their staff.

Also, HR needs to take care of another important requirement of employees – their mental health. It is not surprising that in view of the stress and strain that an employee carries, organizations are working out programs which will render employees fit to face each day at work. Many such measures can be commonly seen in the form of physical fitness programs, dietary training, counselling sessions, sports facilities etc.

c. Change Management – Anything that affects people affects HR and it's the same with Change. HR must focus on change, its effect on people and turning negatives into positives to help employees through the change process. HR must act as change agents and partner with employees as they find their feet through the agonies of transition.

> Your success in life isn't based on your ability to simply change. It is based on your ability to change faster than your competition, customers and business – Mark Sanborn

d. Leadership Development – Effective leadership is one of the foundation stones of any organization's success. HR must set up a process which will ensure that talent with leadership qualities is identified and its skills are developed and honed so that it can take up challenges tomorrow. Ideally, leaders need to come from within the organization and there should be enough scope for them to be trained, developed and their growth.

Challenges in Today's HR Management

> Management is doing things right;
> leadership is doing the right things!
> - Peter F. Drucker

e. Employee Empowerment - Gone are the days when employees waited for orders from their bosses and did as they were told. Market conditions need employees who are able to analyze situations and make decisions on the spot. Obviously, for this an organization needs employees who are 'empowered'. However, this is not a one-time magic potion. It is a culture that needs to percolate in the organization. An organization that authorizes employees and trains them to make decisions and trusts their judgement will have employees who are responsible and able to adapt successfully to changing times.

f. Workforce Adaptability - While it wasn't as if adaptability issues didn't crop up in earlier days, the fact that HR has to handle talent globally, makes workforce adaptability even more crucial today. Today's problems range right from old employees (who have been with the company all their working lives) finding it difficult to adapt to newer people, attitudes, technology and organization structures, to qualified people unable to cope with socio-cultural, economic, psychological or even global differences. When teams today work with people across borders, they are interacting with cultures, languages, values and attitudes that are very different from their own.

HR must ensure that be it technology, processes, skills or people, employees are able to adapt to the demands of the situation. Wherever required, solutions to probable conflicts must be implemented. Where teams interact with others globally, they need to be trained for effective and meaningful communication.

At other places, if employees are not adaptable, HR needs to play a major role, showing employees the bigger picture and reminding them of the bottom line – achievement of organizational goals.

> HR today has to walk the tight-rope between achieving organizational goals and being pro-people.

We - the HR function is about people. Throughout this book, I have tried to give you, the reader a peek into the reality of HR today. It is one of the most dynamic professions in the world which gives you a chance to make a positive difference to people's lives.

Though the factors mentioned in this chapter are challenges that the HR fraternity faces today, they will also be responsible for a sea change in the face of the HR functions in the coming years. Therefore, make sure you as an HR professional are prepared and well-equipped to face these challenges and make your contribution to this rewarding profession.

■■■

Challenges in Today's HR Management

Caselet

Right or Wrong- Who was at fault?

Rakesh had joined the Software Testing department of a renowned IT MNC, three months ago and taken over an important project. He had around 20 years of work experience in software testing. Manish and his team members were between 22-28 years of age and were reporting to Rakesh. Rakesh got along well with Manish and his team. They all were highly motivated and enthusiastic about work and had completed all their tasks on time till date. It was Wednesday afternoon, when Manish (the team leader) and his team members were working on the important project. The deadline was on the same day at 8.00 pm. All team members were working on the same project since the last three months.

When Rakesh entered the cubicles of Manish and his team members around 4.00 pm, he observed that they were chatting on Facebook and Kishore, one of the team members was shopping online. Rakesh got upset as the deadline of the project was at 8.00 pm. He went to the HR department and started shouting at the HR Head mentioning that his staff members were on Facebook and were also shopping online. He was very upset with the HR department as there was no control on the use of social media and e-commerce websites. He did not listen to HR Head's explanation on the same.

Rakesh retuned back to his department and immediately called a meeting with Manish and his team. He shouted at Manish and his team members regarding the use of Facebook and E-commerce websites when urgent work was going on.

They had to submit the project by 8.00 pm that day.

Manish mentioned to Rakesh that it was normal for team members to visit Facebook and E-commerce websites as it worked as a stress buster for everyone. Manish also mentioned that everyone in the team was on the verge of completing the project and would be submitting it before time.

Rakesh was not convinced. He wrote an e-mail to HR to stop the access of such websites for all employees and to issue a memo to the employees who were using Facebook and E-commerce websites during working hours.

Manish and his team completed the work on time and submitted the project. The client sent them an excellent review the next day. Simultaneously, Manish and his team members also received a warning letter from the HR department which would be put in their personnel files with respect to the use of Facebook and social media websites while at work.

What you need to work on:
1. Why was Rakesh annoyed?
2. What is the role of HR in this situation?
3. What should be the reply of Manish and his team?
4. Who was at fault in this scenario?
5. What would you do if you were the HR Head?

Relevant Articles by the Author

❖ Employer & Employee Value Proposition (EVPs) –

• How to foster CREATIVITY in the DNA of the organization?

• What do Corporates expect from Campuses?

• What makes companies a Great Place to work? (Greatness Diaries, September 2014)

❖ The 3 'T's': - Talent Acquisition

Recruitment & Selection –

• Role of Human Capital (Industrial Angles, 2013)

• Dialing into the future (Human Capital HR Magazine, June 2014)

• Being Overqualified - A Myth (Aspiring Minds "Campus Newsletter", October 2012)

Tips for the Interviewee (Candidate) –

• How Long Should Be Your CV? (Timesjob.com)

• Unusual Career Options For Women (Times of India, 2014)

• Why choose a career in Human Resources? (Timesjobs.com, Dec 2013)

• Ideal Resumes (TOI.com, 2013)

❖ Organization Development –

Employee experience -Backbone of Employee productivity (Business Manager)

❖ Exit (Bye Bye) –
• Questions for "Leave Smart, Land Well" research (Survey by Heidrick & Struggles, 2013)

• Tough Decisions without Rough Relationships (Kaustubham TISS 2014)

• Exit with Care

❖ Strategic HR –
• Role of Human Capital (Human Capital, November 2013),

• Cutting Edge or Just a Wedge (Business Manager, December 2013),

• HR as a driver for Organizational Innovation (Information Week, September 2014),

❖ Challenges in Today's Human Resource Management –
Tough Times, Tough Decisions without Rough Relationships (Kaustubham Magazine, TISS, HRM & LR Journal - 2014)

Bibliography

Chapter 2

1. (HR Articles: HR Articles: Difference Between TNA & TNI) http://www.pmiralumni.co.in/2011/06/hr-articles-difference-between-tna-tni.html

2. [PDF]Talent Retention Best Practices - Oracle www.oracle.com/us/media1/talent-retention-6-best-practices-1676595.pdf

3. http://hrcouncil.ca/hr-toolkit/right-people recruitment.cfm

4. The science of talent selection>>Health Management...www.healthmgttech.com/articles/.../the-science-of-talent-selection.php

5. Getting Your Organization Ready for Employee Training ...hrcouncil.ca > ...> HR Toolkit > Learning, Training & Development

6. http://guides.wsj.com/management/managing-your-people/how-to-develop-future-leaders/

7. Human Resource Management- Gary Dessler, Biju, Varkkey

Chapter 3

1. http://www.wisegeek.org/what-is-competency-mapping.htm

2. http://www.thecompetencygroup.com/competency-solutions/competency-assessment.aspx

3. http://www.whatishumanresource.com/competency-

mapping

Chapter 4
1. http://www.schaeferrecognitiongroup.com/
vocationalblog/index.php/2009/10/19/turn-recognition-
expenses-into-profits/

2.http://www.hr.com/en/app/blog/2010/02/compensat
ion-and-benefits-definition-and-importanc_g5kiosxm.html

Chapter 5
1. Organization Development: Principles, Processes,
Performance by Gary N. McLean,
www.bkconnection.com/blog/posts/organizational-
development

2. http://managerlink.monster.com/training-
leadership/articles/189-the-organization-development-
process/
Office of State Personnel, North Carolina

3.https://www.cscollege.gov.sg/Knowledge/Documents/
COD/COD043%20Understanding
%20OD%20and%20its%20Role%20A%20Think%20Piece%
20on%20Organisational%20Development.pdf

4.https://www.cscollege.gov.sg/Knowledge/Pages/Under
standing-OD-and-Its-Role-A-Think-
Piece-on-Organisation-Development.aspx#notes. Author
Christian Chao, Alexia Lee and Geraldine Ling

Chapter 6
CourseiQ – Key Principles of Change Management
www.course-iq.com/blog/?p=394 www.course-

iq.com/blog/?p=394

Chapter 8
(http://www.qualtrics.com/research-suite/employee-exit-interviews/)

Chapter 9
http://www.citehr.com/10060-what-strategic-hr-change-management.html

Chapter 10
1.http://www.researchgate.net/publication/228096231_Challenges_of_Human_Resource_Management_in_borderl ess_world

2. http://www.docstoc.com/docs/86151812/Challenges-before-HR-Managers-in-the-Globalised-Scenario

www.ingramcontent.com/pod-product-compliance
Lightning Source LLC
Chambersburg PA
CBHW021927190326
41519CB00009B/932